Ria's Story
From Ashes to Beauty

Ria Story

Some names and identifying details have been changed to
protect the privacy of individuals.

WHAT READERS ARE SAYING ABOUT RIA'S STORY FROM ASHES TO BEAUTY

"I have actually read this book twice. I took many things in the book and have applied them to my own life. I greatly admire Ria for her strength and in reading this book I found some strength within myself. Thank you Ria for sharing your story." A. Branam

"I'm so delighted Ria has found her voice and is sharing her story...It's so important to speak out about sexual violence to help end the shame, stigma & silence. This important book shows us that there is life after abuse and it's more than possible to have a great life. This book is full of hope & inspiration, and I have nothing but admiration for Ria." Madeleine Black, Author of Unbroken

"A wonderful book by this person who has so much to offer everyone whether they were abused or not." L. Edwards

"I couldn't put this book down; well written and Ria is amazing! Thank you for sharing! She is truly an awesome person!" Kay

"Ria's openness to speak of her unique story is commendable. This is a quick, easy to read true story of a young girl faced with adversity early in her life. Ria is now a strong woman who faced down her past and has overcome it. I recommend reading this inspiring story to anyone who wants reassurance that they can, and will, overcome whatever obstacles life throws their way." M. Watson

"The book is emotional and yet you find yourself thinking, do things like this truly happen to children? The answer: YES it does! This book is an eye opener for everyone! It is an easy read, written in her own words which makes the book come to life." H. Hinsley

"An excellent story of what God can do with any life even after years of hurt and feeling worthless." S. Bird

DEDICATION

I dedicate this book to those who were given ashes.
May God give you healing and hope for
a new tomorrow, as He gave me.

CONTENTS

ACKNOWLEDGMENTS

I would like to thank God.

I would like to thank my husband, family, and friends who have supported me, loved me, and helped me heal.

I would like to thank my mentors and offer a special thanks to Les Brown who spoke into my heart in 2013 when I heard him say, "You have a story someone needs to hear."

1

A NOTE FROM RIA

Everything can be taken from a man but one thing: the last of the human freedoms...to choose one's attitude in any given set of circumstances.

Viktor Frankl

I believe everything happens for a reason. I believe God allows trials and challenges in our lives to help us grow, but He will never give us more than we can bear. I have held firmly to those two beliefs for many years. In my darkest days, there were times when I wanted to give up, and my soul withdrew deep inside while my body was dealing with madness. Days where I could see no way out and no way for things to get better, but I believed they would. I believe we truly have the most wonderful gift from God in the power to choose how we react to the things that happen to us. He has given us the ability to choose our response to any situation and that unique gift means we can live through the trials, challenges and difficult things in life and use them to become stronger and better.

My hope is that sharing with you will help you with your own challenges in life and help you to overcome some obstacles that are holding you back. This isn't really my story – this is God's story living through me. It took me many years to make the difficult decision to share this; but if God can use me to help someone else, then all I can do is prayerfully consider every word written here and ask Him to guide me in the writing of these words.

I realize how blessed I am today. So many people have supported me and lifted me as I have traveled the journey to write this book. After deciding to start sharing my story, it has taken me more than a year to write it down. To pour out my heart on paper realizing once it has been done – I can't take it back.

It hasn't been an easy journey, but then, I know none of us have an easy journey if we are going somewhere worthwhile. Every day, I am reminded how blessed I am to have found a passion for what I do and my purpose in helping others develop. I am reminded how blessed I am to wake up each day excited for what the day holds and how I can make a difference in someone else's life.

Robert Rohm said it well when he asked, "*Is what I am doing right now going to make any difference in my life or in the life of another person today or in eternity?*" What an incredible perspective on how we spend our time and energy. Life is so very precious. The interesting thing about time is that while we can spend it however we choose; we only get to spend it once.

How do we measure our life? When you get to the end of a day or a week and look back, how do you measure whether you have really LIVED those days or not? For me, it is whether I have made a positive difference in someone else's life.

That's a pretty powerful way to measure our actions – Are they actually making a positive difference in our life or someone else's? The best part about this is that it doesn't have to be anything BIG to make a difference. Big actions that make a huge impact are wonderful if and when you can make that happen, but please don't forget the power of making a difference in someone's life by doing something small. I try to make sure I am making a small deposit toward someone every day...Linda Kaplan Thaler wrote about this in her book, *The Power of Small*. She wrote about "*going the extra inch*" – not extra mile or extra 10 feet – but the extra inch. Think with me – what extra inch can you give someone in your life each day for one week? Little things make a big difference!

In February 2010, there were some difficult days for me. Mack, my husband, was traveling frequently. I was alone much of the time while he was away. I would work longer hours and study hard when he was gone, so we could have more fun when he was home. But, I started focusing on what I didn't have rather than focusing on how grateful I was for the blessings I did have. Several weeks went by where I really just walked around in a fog, feeling sorry for myself. I needed to realize how important attitude was and not let my negative attitude pull me down. I was able to work through it and learned to focus on the positive things in life – I had to remind myself to be proactive.

In his book, *Margin*, Dr. Richard Swenson asks: "*If you were handed a 3 x 5 card and asked to write on it one thing you are grateful for, and then another card and another card...How many cards would it take before you ran out of reasons to be thankful? I hope 10,000.*"

How many cards would you need to list all the things you are thankful for? Would you be able to reach 10,000, or would there be cards you should write but don't? I think it's important we don't take for granted the little things in life because little things add up to big things. Having an attitude of gratitude is what keeps us positive and proactive.

In February 2013, I attended John Maxwell's Leadership Certification Training. It was a life-changing week for me. The world of possibilities opened up, and I discovered a passion for coaching others to find their own potential. I discovered there was an entire world of leadership just waiting for me to dive in. I had found a language to communicate the principles I was living out every day. I came out of the three-day event charged up and ready to grow, so I could help other people around me get excited about life!

Mack had signed both of us up for a one-day Les Brown seminar following the JMT event. I didn't know who Les Brown was but quickly learned how inspirational his story was. He earned my respect when he shared the obstacles he has overcome to become one of the top motivational speakers. I will never forget sitting in the audience that day as his words shot through my heart: "*You have a story to tell, and someone in the world needs to hear your story. Only you can help that person – they need you."*

He wasn't talking to me. Or, was he? I think God opened my heart to hear those words and truly consider for the first time there was a reason for all the pain and sadness I had experienced as a teenager. Les Brown planted a seed, but it would be months before that seed sprouted. Returning home, I buried the thought of writing a book or doing any public speaking. I was on a mission of intentional growth – so I could coach other people. I stubbornly refused to consider I should be talking and speaking, so I could share my story and help someone else.

I set a personal deadline – I wanted to be able to pursue a professional coaching career full time in a year. That meant I spent every weekend for the next several months studying the coaching curriculum and developing my listening skill. I was reading, studying, and intentionally growing in personal leadership. What I kept ignoring was that tap on my heart from God that I should be speaking out to help other people discover what I learned early on – we can't control what happens to us in life, but we can control how we respond to it.

Mack and I were blessed to be part of John Maxwell's coaching team that went to Guatemala in June 2013 as part of the Transformation of Guatemala initiative. We were there for a week teaching leadership to thousands of people. What I didn't know was how much the opportunity would help me personally. I paid my own expenses to go to Guatemala, philanthropically thinking I was going to help someone else. What I didn't expect was how the week would transform me. I found a whole new meaning in helping others. One of the things John Maxwell taught us while we were there was success in life pales in comparison to significance. He was right. I couldn't just go back to work the following Monday and appreciate a career – I had found a calling.

Living and teaching leadership to others, both on a personal level and a professional level has helped me grow far beyond what I ever expected. As John C. Maxwell says, *"Everything rises and falls on leadership."* That means how we are leading ourselves as individuals will determine our success and happiness in life. It also means how we are leading ourselves when we interact with others will determine our success and happiness in life.

I was reading recently about Mary and her response when the angel revealed to her God's plan for her (Luke 1:34-55). Her response demonstrated an immediate willingness to serve in accordance with God's plan, which had only just been revealed.

In February 2013, I felt very strongly God was leading me to do something different with my life. I really felt like I was being called to help others, and I felt the gentle tug to start writing this book. I'm not proud of the fact I didn't respond as Mary did immediately *"I am the Lord's servant!"* It took me six months, but I eventually brought my life into alignment with God's plan.

Often, we believe the plan for our life is laid out, and sometimes, we struggle to have an immediate willingness and openness to receive God's plan for our life. I have learned to be more open to God's plans and less dedicated to holding tightly to my own. What's wonderful is the peace I now have in living God's path is far better than anything I would find by insisting on pushing my own way. I am the Lords servant, and I want my life to reflect that - today and every day.

It would be easier for me to let this story go untold forever. It would be easier for me to let the past be forgotten and simply move on with life. Even when victims who have been abused are able to deal with their past, their loved ones must also learn to move on. In a way, I wonder if that is why so many choose to stay silent.

In our society today, we have more social media connections than ever, and yet, we are lonelier than ever when it comes to connecting with people. Why is it that we have so much trouble talking with others about our past? Why is there such a stigma associated with some things like abuse, rape, or even cancer? Why are we afraid to talk about the things we are dealing with in our lives?

My fear had many faces. I feared how my family would feel as I share a story that is not only my story, but theirs as well. I feared some people would blame me for what happened. I feared the guilt I still carry would only become a bigger burden. I feared my husband wouldn't be able to accept the attention sharing my story would bring to our marriage.

There are still many feelings and emotions that overwhelm me at times. Embarrassment, shame, guilt, and a sense of naked vulnerability I don't like to admit. Even today, I am not yet able to openly talk about everything that happened. I probably will never talk about everything that happened.

This isn't a guide to surviving sexual abuse or abuse of any kind. My message to "survivors" of any tragedy is that God doesn't want us to just "survive" what life hands us – he wants us to thrive and live an abundant life. (*"I have come that they may have life and that they may have it more abundantly." John 10:10*)

We can choose to focus on the negative things in our lives or the positive. When we truly understand we choose how we will react to what happens in our lives, we find the true joy of abundant life. Don't ever let the events of your life cause you to miss out on one single moment of happiness. Life is hard – that much is certain. We all have struggles, trials, and difficult things happen to us – some of you have experienced much worse than I have. Lou Holtz said, *"Life is 10% what happens to you, and 90% how you respond to it."*

God gave me a miracle when he brought Mack Story into my life. Mack is strong enough to lift me up when I am feeling down and sensitive enough to pull back when I need time alone. I think God knew I would need help to survive, and He gave me what I needed in the form of a wonderful husband and soul mate. The greatest joy in my life was the day Mack accepted Christ.

I also gained a wonderful relationship with my mother-in-law who has always treated me like a daughter instead of a daughter-in-law. It always surprises me to hear of women who don't like or even appreciate their mother-in-law because I can't imagine life without mine. From the first day she met me, she has wrapped her arms around me and embraced me. I am blessed to know such a special lady.

Sometimes, people ask me how I could possibly

forgive my parents. I learned a long time ago I needed to do that in order to move on with my life. Forgiving other people is part of our own personal growth journey - we must choose to move forward down the path rather than backwards. Is there someone in your life you need to forgive? Is there something you need to let go of in order to move forward?

It makes me sad to think there is no way to repair the deep abyss that destroys some relationships. While I do not have a relationship with either of my parents, I do have peace in realizing I have been able to move beyond any feelings of betrayal or hurt. I hope and pray they too have found peace. I found forgiveness in my heart. Extending forgiveness is something we need to do to let go of any feelings of anger, blame, or vindictiveness. If someone breaks trust, it is an opportunity for us to grow in our ability to be a better person and forgive a wrong done. I have no desire to cause them, or anyone else, pain.

This is the moment I have been dreading and looking forward to all at the same time for years. One of the most difficult things I've ever done is write this book. It's like opening your heart to the world and simply praying someone will benefit from it. This is the day I have decided I can tell my story, my way, in my words. I still struggle with guilt that I should have done or been something different. My hope and prayer is I can help someone by sharing my journey. My prayer for you, as you read this, is that you can find peace like I did when I decided not to run from the past but to embrace it as part of what made me who I am today. This brings purpose to the pain and is reason enough to share what I would rather have left behind forever. Our scars make us stronger.

We are all created in the image of God -yet, we are our own creation as well because God gave us the gift of choice. We make our own choices and must live with the consequences. Here is my story and some of my choices...right or wrong, they are what made me who I am today. And for that, I am grateful.

2

THE STRENGTH TO SHARE

Life isn't a matter of milestones, but of moments.

Rose Kennedy

August 2013. I was sitting in a hotel in Orlando, Florida. I was attending a Les Brown Speaker Training event I had signed up for in February. Or rather, Mack had signed me up, ignoring my protests that we didn't need to spend the money. I didn't want to be a speaker anyway. But, there I was. We had attended the John Maxwell Certification conference the first part of the week. We had been in Orlando several days already, and these last two days of the Speaker Training event were winding up our weeklong trip.

I was sitting at the table with several people I didn't know, while listening to the instructions we were being given for the following day. When we signed up for this event in February, we were told Les Brown was going to select five finalists from this event to speak on stage with him at a future event. Everyone listened eagerly to know what he or she needed to do.

We were going to be given one minute each to present our story to the group at our table the following morning. The people at our table would vote for one table winner, who would advance to the next round and speak from the stage for the judges. Of those approximately 35 people, 10 would be chosen by a panel to move to the final round and give their one-minute speech to the entire audience. Five of those would be selected as the winners.

I wrote down the instructions even though I didn't need to. They were simple: A one-minute speech on a topic of our choice. I gathered my things and said good evening to my tablemates while scanning the room for Mack and my mother-in-law Joanne. I found them still engaged in conversations, so I sat nearby to wait, wrapped up in my own thoughts.

I had already decided the topic for my speech – I decided it six months ago in February when Mack signed me up for the August training. I wasn't the least bit nervous about speaking either. That didn't bother me really; after all, I had been speaking in front of people on a regular basis in my role at the hospital and as a group fitness instructor.

What was on my mind was the story I wanted to tell. I wanted to share *my* story because I believed Les Brown was speaking to me when he said, *"You have a story, and someone needs to hear it."*

I was afraid. I was afraid telling my story would

change how people look at me and what they think about me. I was afraid some people would talk to me about it, and I was afraid some people wouldn't talk to me about it.

We had dinner that evening with several friends who were attending the training. Everyone was strategizing and sharing about their speeches for the next day. Everyone, except me. I kept saying I wasn't sure about my topic yet, and I needed to think more about it. A quote from Eleanor Roosevelt kept running through my head, "*I am who I am today because of the choices I made yesterday.*"

I had this quote taped to the hutch over my desk at work. I looked at it every day and knew it by heart. Repeating it to myself all through dinner, I realized I was planning to talk about my past choices. At that moment, I was making a choice that would affect the rest of my life. I often thought about that quote and considered how it meant the choices I made in the past affect who I am now. Suddenly, I realized it also means the choices I make today and tomorrow will affect who I will be in the future.

After dinner, Mack, Joanne and I worked together on their speeches. I helped them, offering tips, typing up the script until they were comfortable and ready. I kept telling them I would be fine with my own speech. I just needed to practice by myself a few times and would be ready. Around midnight, I was feeling pretty good about how well they were doing and decided they could fine tune without me. I grabbed my laptop and told them I was going to find a quiet place to practice.

Too self-conscious to practice with them, I found a

quiet chair near the lobby and typed up my speech. It only took about two minutes to type it up. Then, I sat there and stared at my laptop. I whispered my speech to myself a few times – afraid to say it out loud. I worked on the words again, refining it and making it clean. 60 seconds isn't much time to make a point, so I kept cutting it down. Satisfied, I went back to the room about 1:00am.

The next thing I knew my phone alarm was ringing for a 4:00am wake up call. I grabbed it and switched it off quickly, so I wouldn't wake up Mack. In the dark, I found my running shoes and went outside for a run. I ran for about 30 minutes, repeating my speech over and over to myself as I ran. After about three miles, I stopped and looked around. I was close to the hotel golf course, and it was deserted. I took a deep breath and finally said my one-minute speech out loud. It took 46 seconds. Perfect! I knew it would take a little longer on stage, and I didn't want to go over. I said it again a few more times, practicing to make sure I could say it before I turned around to head back.

At 5:15am, I quietly tiptoed back into the hotel room to shower and dress. Mack was still asleep when I left the room again in search of a large cup of coffee. I needed to practice somewhere quiet. I found a corner in the convention center of the hotel and used my laptop to video myself repeatedly until I felt like I had it exactly right.

At 9:30am, a friend found me. We started chatting. She mentioned she was concerned about running out of time, so I offered to time her. She practiced. Then offered, *"Okay, let me time you now."* I was not prepared but reluctantly agreed it would be helpful. I broke into tears while giving my speech. It took almost two minutes to get the words out. She hugged me and wished me luck. I knew I had to get my emotions under control.

I sat down on a sofa near the ladies room after repairing my mascara. Shaking and emotional, the only thing I knew to do was pray. *"Lord, if this is your will, then give me the strength to do this. If it's not your will, then lay another topic on my heart for this speech."*

With a sense of peace, I felt better and went back to the conference area. At exactly 10:00am, the doors to the conference room opened; we went in and found our seats. The room felt electric with energy. The first hour of the conference passed quickly with some fun activities to get us creatively engaged.

We were given a countdown clock. The time for us to present to our individual tables had come. Since I went first yesterday with introductions, Steve, on my right, went first this time. He shared his one-minute speech, and I was touched.

The next person went. Then, it was my turn. I stood and waited for the countdown clock. Then, I blurted out my speech, rushing through it and hoping no one was really paying attention. But, they were. Everyone hugged me when I was done, saying I had done a good job. The rest of our group finished with their speeches. I think everyone was glad it was over.

Now, the time had come to vote on who would advance to the next round. There were five of us at the table, but only two of us were eligible for the next round, Steve and I. Again, I took a moment to pray and wrote down my vote for Steve on my slip of paper. Lareece, on my left, counted the votes; three for me and two for Steve. Steve told me he was proud of me. I was grateful for his kind words.

The table winners were asked to stay while everyone else went to lunch. I looked around the room. There were 35 other people sitting at their own tables. I knew most of them, at least by name. Our instructions were brief: come up on stage and give your one-minute speech. I sat there, inspired and amazed as the talented speakers presented. We clapped for everyone. There was a strong sense of support from the group. Sitting at the very back of the room, I was one of the last to go.

One last prayer, I asked God to give me strength. I made my way to the stage and picked up the microphone. This was my last chance to change my mind. More than anything, I just wanted it to be over. For the first time, I was going to share my story publicly. I nodded for my countdown timer.

"Eleanor Roosevelt said, 'I am who I am today because of the choices I made yesterday.' 13 years ago, I decided I wasn't going to let seven years of sexual abuse hold me back. I was 19 when I left home. Don't let the past hold you back. You are who you are today because of the choices you made yesterday. But, who you will be tomorrow is based on the choices you make today. Choose wisely."

3

THE LOSS OF INNOCENCE

Life is a succession of lessons which must be lived to be understood.

Helen Keller

I went to a private, Christian, kindergarten at four years old. After that, my parents made the decision to homeschool my brother and me. There were a few families, other homeschoolers, who we were friends with and did some educational activities with over the years. But overall, it was lonely growing up. Homeschooling today is much different. Now, there are many ways for homeschooling families to have their kids involved in activities.

I was seven years old when my parents bought 100 acres of land and moved far from the city in order to start a farm. Living so far out and not attending church or school meant we were very isolated most of the time.

I treasured the opportunities we had to get together with friends. I would look forward to those occasions for weeks beforehand. An annual camping trip to Florida was a special treat around the end of October since we didn't celebrate Halloween. We didn't celebrate many holidays because Dad thought they were satanic. We also didn't believe in Santa Claus, the Tooth Fairy, or the Easter Bunny because they were *"just make believe."*

Dad was an absolute ruler in his world. He had strict rules for everyone. Once a week, we would travel into town to visit family or friends, buy groceries, and run errands. We weren't allowed to be gone from home past 5:00pm except on very rare, special occasions.

I wasn't allowed to go swimming anywhere in public or anywhere boys were around. I loved gymnastics, but Dad decided when I was seven it wasn't ladylike and made me quit. I joined a Girl Scouts Troop, but Dad thought they were a bad influence on me, so he made me quit. I started going to a Girls in Action group with a friend whose church started a chapter, but Dad thought it was too much religion and made me quit that too. I also took flute lessons for a while. My Grandfather would drive all the way out to get me, take me to the lesson, and then take me home. I kept doing that as long as I could, just to drive my Dad crazy because he didn't want me to go. Eventually, that stopped too.

Once, when I was about 13 or 14, my grandparents took my brother and me to the "YMCA." I didn't have a bathing suit to wear. My Grandmother bought me one, and we went swimming. There was hell to pay when we got back home. My Dad was angry at my Grandmother for buying me a bathing suit and angry at me for wearing it. It didn't occur to me then to lie about it. I just accepted my punishment.

I wasn't allowed to cut my hair - because *"A woman's hair is for the glory of God."* My mother didn't work outside the home except once when I was very young. She worked plenty on the farm and in the cabinet shop we had. She either wasn't permitted or didn't want to work outside and earn an actual income. Looking back now, it seems as if it was another way to control her. Hearing her beg over and over for grocery money or maybe a few dollars for some new clothes made a huge impression on me as I was growing up. I was determined to be independent and self-supporting when I grew up, so I wouldn't have to beg like she did.

We grew some of our food on the farm. We had chickens for meat and eggs, goats for milk, and rabbits for meat. I remember the first time I had to slaughter a chicken. I was 10 years old, and I got sick afterward from the blood and mess. Dad thought it was important that my brother and I were able to be self-sufficient.

We also had dogs and cats. There were too many cats to vaccinate or neuter, and it wasn't unusual for 20 or more cats to be outside the house.

The chickens were my responsibility, and I was allowed to keep the money from selling the eggs to help pay for my horses. I was in love with horses from an early age and got my first pony when I was nine. For several years, until I left home, I raised gaited horses and trained them for show.

My Dad was a gun enthusiast and also believed there was a governmental conspiracy against him. He kept a small stockpile of guns and ammunition in case his second amendment rights were threatened. I don't believe we ever had health insurance or car insurance, even when the law was passed stating you had to have car insurance. Dad believed you didn't need insurance when you had God. He also didn't believe in paying taxes because he said the government was so corrupt.

I was 12 when Dad started having some conversations with me about the *"facts of life."* He would tell me how infidelity in marriage was wrong and so was divorce. But, *"his needs"* weren't being met because my mother wasn't able to meet them. I was told they didn't have a physical relationship for many years, but I don't know if that is true. I know she was sleeping on the couch in the living room most nights, she said because of her back. I suspect I will never know the truth. I want to believe she had no idea what was going on, but it's possible she knew and didn't want to face reality, so she shut it out. Either version is hard for me to accept, but there are many things in life we don't want to accept.

I remember times when Mom was gone, out running errands or something, and my Dad would tell her to take my brother with her. At first, all our talks were about how I needed to be *"pure"* and stay away from boys until my Dad was able to find the *"Right one that God would send."* Then, it changed to being all about how a woman was designed by God to meet a man's needs and that was all I was created for. I remember feeling ashamed talking about things like that, but I didn't know what to do. It was the summer when I was 12 that he first started saying how a father-daughter relationship was supposed to be close in every way, physically as well as emotionally. I remember being told I was supposed to give my heart to him *"for safekeeping,"* but I was confused as to why that also meant in a physical way.

One day my Mom and brother were gone and Dad and I were sitting in the living room *"talking."* Somehow, things turned into how wonderful it was that I was the perfect daughter and was so close to my Dad. We went upstairs, and he kept telling me how God intended for daughters to belong to daddies. And, if I would trust him, he would make sure I lived up to what God wanted. He told me how I was supposed to fill in since my Mother wasn't able to be a wife anymore. He told me I was living up to God's purpose for my life by helping him not have to commit adultery. He told me it wasn't a sin if I helped him like that. He took off my clothes and told me the whole time I was the perfect daughter.

What started out as just taking off my clothes progressed. Within a few months, it wasn't just taking off my shirt and jeans but taking off everything.

Deep in the back of a forgotten drawer, my Mom had hidden a bunch of lingerie she used to wear when she was young, and they were newly married. Dad brought it out one day while we were alone in the house together. He picked out one of the outfits and told me to go in the bathroom. Then, he wanted me to put it on and come out to model it for him. I cried afterward, ashamed of being looked at like that. I was sad for my Mom too - her personal things should not have been shared with anyone, much less her daughter.

Then, the touching started. At first, it was just him touching me. But then, I was shown how I needed to touch him too.

It wasn't long before I started having nightmares. I remember one morning, I woke up in tears. That was the day I begged him not to tell anyone what we were doing. By that point, I was convinced what we were doing wasn't right, but no one would believe me. I begged him to never tell my Mother what we were doing. I was so worried it would hurt her.

I look back now and wonder why on earth no one ever said anything. This went on for years. If you look at pictures of me growing up, especially with friends, I was always dressed in revealing clothes Dad would buy for me. I can remember being made to sit on his lap even when I was 15, 16 and older. My heart cries when I think there are other young people going through something similar, and no one ever wants to rock the boat by saying something. If we stand by and do nothing, we are simply allowing it to happen.

Dad soon started bargaining with me whenever I wanted something. If I needed horse feed, I would ask for money to buy it, and he would refuse to give it to me until I did something to please him sexually. If I wanted to do something with a friend, I had to earn the right by letting him "tuck me in" at night.

Deep down, I knew it was wrong, and it would devastate my mother. But, I thought I was helping her by keeping him happy. All I wanted was some peace for them. They fought so often - yelling and screaming at each other for just the smallest thing. If Mom happened to be coming home at 5:01pm instead of 4:58pm, there was a fight. The rule was 5:00pm, and that meant to the minute. If she forgot to do something, there was a fight. I think she wasn't really capable of running a household, a farm, and a home business and had the tendency to just have a crying fit at the smallest thing, screaming at the top of her lungs that life was over for her.

My Dad built houses and did construction work. We also had a business selling products for other homeschoolers. I remember one time, we were packing to leave for a sales convention. My Mom had a complete meltdown because she couldn't find the directions to get to the conference. She sat in the floor screaming and crying that my Dad would kill her for not getting there on time and selling products. I was 16 and had learned to shut out her emotional outbursts and focus on what had to be done.

Ignoring her crying on the floor, I called the convention hosts from the previous year and simply asked for the contact for the current year, so I could get directions. Mom sat on the floor and stared at me while I made the call and calmly wrote down where we needed to go.

I think she simply wasn't able to function normally, a fact which I believe contributed to my feelings of responsibility. I am only 14 months older than my brother and automatically started assuming duties like household chores in my teenage years. If for no other reason, because I needed clean clothes to wear, and Mom just wasn't able to get things done.

I look back now and wonder if it was something small that a prescription could have helped. But whatever the reason, she wasn't able to cope with the demands of life. She was gifted in many other areas and was especially creative. I remember her sewing amazing projects like fabric mallard ducks that were life sized and very real looking. She made beautiful smocked dresses and creatively decorated cakes too. Growing up, I thought she was beautiful inside and out.

Our home was always full of turmoil, so I learned to withdraw within myself and seek out solitude and silence when I could. I would ride my horse into the woods with some snacks and a paperback book. I would sit and read for hours, propped up against a pine tree.

It was just days past my 17th birthday when I discovered the World Wide Web. We had recently gotten our desktop computer hooked up to the internet. Those were the early days of internet - dial up connections and AOL version 2.0. I stayed up late and ended up getting on the computer. Figuring things out wasn't hard - I created my own AOL account and felt like I was really grown up because I had my own account. I stayed up most of the night surfing the web and discovering chat rooms.

Life was transformed in an instant. All of a sudden, my world expanded infinitely. I never realized, until that point, that I was a social person. But suddenly, I had the world at my keyboard! I could connect with hundreds of people. Faceless and via the web, interacting with others was suddenly simple - an open door which I bolted through as fast as possible. Within weeks, I was trying to connect with other people who were local and the inevitable happened - I found someone.

He was about a two hour drive away but willing to drive down in the middle of the night to meet me. Warning bells should have been ringing, but my alarm system had been disconnected. I had been hearing for years my purpose in life was to make a man happy, my father. Yet, I yearned to find something more.

At 17, I had no standard of normal and very little self-respect. My relationship with my father had progressed to the point of almost nightly sessions where I was forced to do almost everything except actual intercourse. I had nothing to lose and nothing to fear. Hearing daily I was destined to only marry when Dad found someone suitable, I was half-crazy with thoughts I would be living my entire life under those circumstances.

In June of 1998, I finally met my online "friend." I snuck out of the house in the middle of the night. What started out as just talking and having fun ended up in rape. It wasn't much different than what my father had been doing to me, and I shouldn't have been surprised. But, I felt my trust had been violated as much as anything. In the end, I cried, but my "friend" told me to toughen up. I crawled back into my house in the early morning hours before dawn and cried myself to sleep.

In September, with my 18th birthday coming up in just one month, I was depressed. As a special birthday treat, my Dad planned a trip with me. A special trip – just the two of us. I knew what was coming by that time.

We have an amazing ability to cope with what life hands us. I remember that trip only a little. My Dad took me to eat at Hardee's before checking in to the motel and raping me. I don't remember where we were or anything else about the trip.

I shut down emotionally and disconnected, which may not be healthy but is a sure defense mechanism when you are slowly dying inside. We build walls sometimes in our hearts in order to keep who we are deep down inside safe. That is what I did. For me, I thought it was the only way to survive. I was simply numb – there wasn't anything left to feel.

4

A LOST SOUL

To love means loving the unlovable. To forgive means pardoning the unpardonable. Faith means believing the unbelievable. Hope means hoping when everything seems hopeless.

Gilbert K. Chesterton

My life went from bad to worse. Within weeks of the rape, I was given a wedding ring to wear whenever we were in public, but not around family. I felt like a piece of property, and I was emotionally blackmailed into going along with everything. I was convinced I was supposed to think my purpose in life was to make my father happy. Yet deep down, I was struggling because I knew it wasn't right. I would cry myself to sleep many nights and try to be tough during the day. Dad was a master at manipulating my emotions to make me feel sorry for him and then guilty for trying to stop him. He always said the only way he was going to be able to go to Heaven was if I didn't tell anyone what was going on. If I told, that meant he would go to Hell, so it was my responsibility to make sure he wasn't condemned eternally.

He spent endless hours *"talking"* to me, while I studied the wallpaper patterns and tried to shut everything out. I learned to just shut down emotionally and retreat to a secret place inside my heart. My safe place.

Several months after the birthday trip, I was informed my *"education"* wasn't complete. I needed to experience more before I was married and committed to one man for the rest of my life. My objections were overruled, and I simply stopped fighting or saying no. Every time I tried, he would convince me I had caused him to sin horribly, everything was my fault, and he would go to hell. After a few hours of that, I would cave in and agree to whatever it was he was considering and agree it was God's will. He started searching for other people (men and women) that would help me expand my horizons.

I was always introduced as his wife. Although looking back now, I can't imagine why no one questioned that. Maybe they did, and I never knew it. I looked older than 19 but certainly not old enough to be married to someone who was over 40.

One night in a bar, we met a married couple who wanted to have sex with another female and would let the male watch. After that meeting, the couple decided not to "play" with us, and that was fine with me.

One time, I was taken to an amusement park, at night, where we met an older man. I was told he was married to a disabled woman who wasn't able to have sex. I was told God had provided me to him, so he wouldn't have to commit adultery. I was forced to perform oral sex on him in a storage room behind one of the park attractions. Later, I learned he worked there, and the whole situation had been set up, so I wouldn't know his real name.

I was also shared with several different men who were allowed to have sex with me while my Dad watched.

One time, my Dad took me to Florida. We met a man there and booked a hotel room. They took me to a restaurant for dinner, dressed me up in revealing clothing, and called me *"slave"* during the whole meal. After dinner, we went back to the hotel, and they both took turns having sex with me. That night, I was tied up, photographed nude, beaten with a riding crop until bruised all over from waist to knees, hung from the ceiling, gagged, and forced to perform sexual acts. They kept trying to make me cry out and beg for it to stop. But, I wouldn't give in. I was holding on to a shred of pride by refusing to beg.

I obediently participated physically and shut down emotionally to deal with what was happening. The bruises healed within a few weeks. The emotional wounds took much longer.

In a self-destructive pattern, I continued to seek out people on the Internet. Fascinated by the possibilities and forbidden interactions with society, I was staying up every night, nearly all night, in order to be online.

Somehow, I convinced my Dad I needed my own computer in my room. That just made it worse. I figured out I could buy pre-paid calling cards or accept calls without the charges showing up on the phone bill. I was brilliant in the schemes I thought up, but I kept digging a deeper hole.

I thought my only escape was the Internet "friends" I was making. I longed for a normal life, but I was forbidden to date at all. I was 18 years old. I had never been to school, we didn't attend regular church anymore, and I only had a couple of friends at that point.

I was pretty much free to do what I wanted at home while Dad was at work. I would play bridge online, visit chat rooms, read, ride horses, and pretend I was normal.

One day, I was sitting at the computer, and I just started crying for no reason. I couldn't stop crying. I remember thinking I was lost forever. Why would God allow such terrible things to happen to me? I was living a life of sin and lies, and I knew that road wouldn't take me any place good. In my despair, I felt hopeless, and I couldn't see any way that I would ever be able to get out of my situation. The thought crossed my mind that I could just end it all. I had read about someone who committed suicide by slitting their wrists, and it was supposed to be painless. It would have been easy at that moment. I believe there was an angel sitting on my shoulder who helped me push that thought away. There is always hope when you have faith.

I had been baptized when I was 16. We studied scripture together as a family and sometimes had church services at the house. During this period of my life however, I wasn't close to God. I had no idea then how a close relationship with God would have helped me so much through those years of my life. I felt like God was too far away to pay attention to me. I felt dirty, ashamed, and afraid God wouldn't want me.

I had no one to confide in. I treasured the few friends I had, but yearned for one I could really confide in completely. I knew that would be a mistake however, so I kept my awful secret.

I was thoroughly trained – if anyone asked me, I was supposed to say my heart belonged to my father, and I wasn't interested in dating or marriage. I expected that eventually he would choose whomever I would be married to, if ever. By this point, I was numb to what was happening to me. My Dad's favorite thing to say was how one day he wanted my future husband to thank him for how much he had taught me about how to *be a good wife.*

On the surface, life was great. I was playing bridge with the local bridge club and even traveled a little for bridge tournaments. I'm sure some friends may have been envious. I had horses. We had a pool. I had my own cell phone, which was expensive in those days. I didn't have to work. I didn't have to go to college or school, and I even had my own car.

What no one saw was I didn't have what every one of us need and want: freedom, safety, and security. I constantly had to worry about talking to a young man and the consequences if my Dad found out.

One time, my brother and I were guests of some friends who took us water skiing at a local ski club. One of the guys there was very friendly, and at some point during the day while talking to me, patted my shoulder. My brother innocently told my Dad about it. Dad became furious with me. I wasn't allowed to go back for a long time, even though I really enjoyed it and there was nothing inappropriate going on.

Emotionally, I was imploding. I ran away from home three times during the year when I was 18, desperate for anyone to save me and keep me from having to go back. Each time, Dad would find me and take me back, using emotional blackmail to get me to agree to go back and continue living at home.

One time, he took me to a tent revival after catching me and asked them to lay hands on me to save me from Satan and keep me from wanting to leave home again. That experience scared me to death as my formal religious experiences up to that point were fairly conservative. I was now convinced I was going to hell for trying to leave against my father's wishes.

I still have guilt about my actions during that time of my life – I am certainly not proud of my behavior and mistakes. There is so much I wish I could change. Whether or not it would condemn me to hell, I became determined to get out. I started saving a little bit of money in a stash, so when I got out, I would have something. I had no idea what it would cost to get going in life. Looking back now, it was silly how I thought the few dollars I managed to hide would be enough to save me. However, it helped me feel like I had a plan – maybe it wasn't a good one, but I had a plan. God had a better plan – I just didn't know it yet.

So much of what happens to us in life is difficult to deal with. I love the quote by Joseph Newton, "*People are lonely because they build walls instead of bridges."* If there is pain in your life today, look for a way to build a bridge to someone instead of building a wall and keeping them out. Sometimes, we can't even talk about our painful experiences in life. Sometimes, there are no words to say and no language to speak because what happened is still unspeakable. We can't rush the process of sharing those moments - sometimes they will never be shared. But, we can open our heart to someone and let their friendship help us heal. We cannot be afraid of opening up to a friend.

When we open our hearts, we become vulnerable. Yet, we can't let that stop us. If we do, we miss out on the opportunity. It takes courage to step forward and connect with someone, but as Nelson Mandela said, *"I learned that courage was not the absence of fear, but the triumph over it. The brave man is not he who does not feel afraid, but he who conquers fear."*

From Ashes To Beauty

5

FINDING A FRIEND

Sometimes it's the smallest decisions that can change your life forever.

Keri Russell

It was a hot summer night in Alabama. June 2000. I drove north on the interstate headed to the city. My best friend, Autumn, sat in the seat beside me. We were laughing and talking. She called a friend to see where we should eat dinner that night. I had told my parents we were going X-treme bowling with some friends, so we could stay out late. We were headed to a club Autumn had heard about, so we could hang out.

I was nervous but excited – I didn't get out of the house much. This was going to be fun! We ended up having dinner at a local restaurant and went out to a club downtown. There wasn't anyone there because we were so early, but we didn't have anything else to do. Autumn had just broken up with her boyfriend. She was ready for some fun. We were both 19, but she had a fake ID. I didn't really drink, so I didn't care that I was driving that night. I had changed into something I thought was cute after leaving the house. I knew my Dad wouldn't approve of me wearing that outfit when he wasn't around, but I didn't care. I was determined to try to be normal.

Stepping into the dark club, music was going, but nobody was dancing yet. Autumn grabbed me by the hand, *"Let's go outside."*

We walked outside to the little side court and stood there. Ever the social one, she started chatting to some of the bouncers. I smiled and nodded but didn't say much. I noticed one guy was a little quiet. But, he seemed friendly.

The crowd started drifting into the club, and the noise picked up. Autumn was all into the crowd, talking to a bunch of guys, and dancing with different ones. I envied her confident social skills. She and I got separated, but that was okay. I talked briefly to one guy, Mr. Pushy, who said, *"Let's dance to the next song."* I agreed, not thinking I could say no. He ducked to the bar first for another beer. I stood by the wall and waited. The quiet guy I had seen earlier walked up and actually started to talk to me.

Awkward and shy, I managed to stumble out a few words and kicked myself mentally for not being talkative and cute like Autumn. Mr. Pushy returned from the bar and grabbed my hand. I took two steps away before turning around to tell my quiet friend I would be right back. It never occurred to me I had a right to say, *"No, I don't want to dance."* But, Mr. Quiet was gone when I turned around, apparently thinking I was not interested. Frustrated, I let myself be pulled to the dance floor with Mr. Pushy who was drunk, getting obnoxious, and way too friendly. Desperate, I looked around but couldn't find Autumn. Mentally, I sighed and tried to think of a nice way to get away from Mr. Pushy. Suddenly, Mr. Quiet tapped me on the shoulder, *"Your friend wants you outside."* I was saved!

I turned around and left Mr. Pushy alone on the dance floor, thankful for a chance to get outside from the smoke and noise. Mr. Quiet led me outside where Autumn had taken a chair around a table with some other people. She was having fun. I pulled up a chair, grateful to be outside in the fresh air. Mr. Quiet turned to leave, apparently deciding his job in reuniting me with my friend was done.

"Wait, where are you going? You can sit down." I called out - desperate for him to stay but not sure how to say it. I was surprised though; he said, *"Okay"* and pulled up another chair. Thinking to myself, *"Wow this guy is kind of nice,"* I tried to be conversational. As usual, I wasn't sure what to say. It must have been enough though - he asked if he could call me.

"Um, no. But, I'll call you." I replied, as always, evasive about myself. *"Or, email you. Do you have email?"*

"Uh, yeah sure, that's fine." He replied and pulled out a business card. I have to admit I was impressed. Who goes to a club with business cards? We talked for a while, and it wasn't long before *"Brown Eyed Girl"* started

playing. I couldn't keep my foot from tapping. *"You want to dance?"* he asked me. *"Yes!"* That was perfect – I wouldn't have to worry about talking. He led me to the dance floor, and I started dancing to the beat. *"Can I touch you?"* He asked me. *"I mean, is it okay? I don't want to offend you."*

I wasn't sure how else you could dance with someone without at least touching hands, but I was impressed to be asked first. *"Yes, sure."* I replied.

We finished the song. Soon, it was time to go. Autumn and I found our way to the car. I stopped at Waffle House before getting on the interstate, so I could change clothes again. It was a long drive home. It was late when I pulled into the yard and parked away from the house. Autumn and I snuck inside. I was glad my parents had already gone to bed. I tucked the card away in a special place where I was sure my Dad wouldn't find it, and we went to sleep.

Little did I know, that night would change my life forever.

It was the first Saturday in September, 2000. Labor day weekend was coming up and of course the three-day holiday. I had told my parents I was spending the weekend with my friend Autumn at her Dad's house in North Alabama, and she was going to cover for me if needed. I was really going to spend the weekend with Mr. Quiet, who turned out to be Mack Story.

He seemed like a really nice guy. We had been sending emails back and forth and even talked on the phone several times. I had stopped by to see him a couple of times, but I never would reveal where I lived or even my full name. One day, he demanded I show him my driver's license, so he could be sure I was really 19 years old. He wasn't sure about the secrecy but was getting tired of it pretty quickly. I was a little nervous about that. I didn't want to mislead him, but I couldn't reveal the truth of my circumstances to him.

Saturday afternoon was great and went by in a blur. We went out to eat and had some fun together laughing and talking. Sunday was a little quieter. I could tell something was on Mack's mind. Sometime after dark, we were talking. He was talking, and I was listening. I couldn't believe what I was hearing. He started telling me he knew what was going on, that I was being abused by my Dad, but it was okay; it wasn't my fault, and he could help me get out of there and go somewhere else.

I just started to cry. In 19 years, no one had ever held me and said, *"It will be okay, it's not your fault."* I couldn't deny it any longer. I cried and cried. That was answer enough for him. He suddenly stood up and left the room, yelling with frustration and hurt for me. Stunned, I just sat there and asked myself what I had done - I had given away the secret. The secret I wasn't supposed to tell anybody. The secret I had begged my Dad not to tell anyone because I was ashamed. I decided I would lie about it and deny it. If Mack couldn't keep the secret, I would tell him it wasn't true.

When he came back to me, he hugged me, said he was sorry for leaving and being mad, and that I was the one who was hurt. I was shocked by the sympathy, surprised not to be the one held to blame for it. I knew deep down it was shameful. Mack had guessed a little bit, but he didn't know for sure. He had no idea how lost I had been for years and years. We stayed up almost all night talking, crying together, and hugging. I silently thanked God for him, and I found comfort in the knowledge that for just a little while at least, I was safe. By the time early morning arrived, I had started to think about reality. It was Monday, and I had to go home.

"Oh no. You aren't going back there." Mack told me. "I'll take you anywhere else you want to go, but I can't let you go back to that house, and if you do, I will call the police." I gave that some thought. An encounter with the police was the last thing I wanted. I simply wanted to crawl into a hole and disappear without talking to anyone at all.

Mack didn't know it yet, but I had already tried to leave home by running away three times, unsuccessfully. Every time, my Dad came after me, found me, and took me back. The last time, I made it all the way to my grandparent's house. They were going to let me stay there for a while, not knowing why I was so upset but trying to help. My Mother had come and tried to "talk some sense into me." She begged me to just take a car ride with her, but once inside the car, she started screaming how I was killing my Dad by running away, and it was my fault he would die. I tried to jump out of the car at a red light. She nearly wrecked when she swerved as we struggled. I was determined not to go back. Then, they took my Dad to the emergency room that night with chest pains.

Once again, I felt like I was the one to blame. So, I agreed to go back. I told myself I could be strong and if I just tried harder things would be better. Christmas came three days later, and I pretended I was happy. I don't think anyone believed me, especially my grandparents. I was forcing myself to laugh and pretend I was fine, so we could have a normal Christmas as a family. I wasn't fine – I was dying inside the whole time.

After giving it some thought and talking about it, Mack and I decided I would stay with him. I knew better than to go back to my grandparent's house. They meant well, but I wasn't going to tell them the truth, and I knew my parents would come after me again like before. I thought if I had Mack to protect me they would stay away, and I decided I wasn't going to tell them where I was. The problem with that plan was I had no clothes or anything. I called Autumn and told her I was leaving home, and I needed her help. She agreed to sneak back into my house with me and help me get some clothes and stuff.

There are many people who will call themselves your friend, but won't stick around when you ask for help. A true friend will care enough to help you out, even if it means they take a risk. A true friend will stand up for you.

I believe to this day angels were with us. We drove up to my house and parked without the dogs barking. We managed to walk boldly in the back door in broad daylight and upstairs to my room. Once there, I shut the door and almost panicked. Autumn never missed a beat. She pulled out a duffle bag from the closet and stuffed it with clothes. When that was full, she pulled off my pillowcases from the bed and stuffed them too. I kept trying to leave, but she kept insisting we get more of my clothes. *"You are going to need this coat, sister, when it gets cold."* I remember her insisting I choose a coat, which seemed ridiculous in the 90-degree heat and Alabama humidity. We hurriedly finished and crept downstairs.

As we walked out the back door, I risked a look towards the living room. My Dad was sitting right there with his back to us. How he hadn't heard the noise upstairs I will never know, except I do believe in God's protection. I know if he had caught us, I wouldn't have had the courage to leave.

Autumn and I made a clean get away. My cell phone started ringing shortly after, but I wouldn't answer it. I didn't want to talk to my parents. Certain they would try to find me, I asked Autumn to call them once I was safely back in Auburn and tell them I was okay, but I wasn't coming home. By that time, I had shared a little of my circumstances with her. She was mad enough to be firm with my parents and tell them I wasn't coming back home. Ever. We parked my car in town nearby, and she told my parents where to pick it up. I didn't want to owe them a thing, and the car was in my Mom's name anyway.

I piled my pillowcases of clothes in Mack's Camaro. We loaded it up. Then, we stopped at his mother's house. I remember feeling bad because she cooked dinner, but I couldn't eat. I was emotionally drained and really just wanted some time to be alone.

The next few weeks were a roller coaster. I refused to talk to my parents at all, and I barely talked to my grandparents, afraid to tell the truth. I was still struggling with shame and guilt, and I didn't want anyone to know.

A few weeks after I left, my Mom suddenly showed up at Mack's home where we were living. They had tracked his number from my cell phone records and found his name and address. She stood outside and shouted until I finally let her in. I didn't tell her anything, although she cried and pleaded with me to tell her why I suddenly left home. She visited once a week for about three more weeks. Each time she came, she would bring me something from home and take me to eat somewhere, so we could talk. I wanted her to bring my dog Solomon, but Mack and I had no room for a large dog. I knew I wouldn't be able to keep him.

On her third visit after lunch, she sat with me in the living room and begged one more time for me to talk. She promised she would always love me, and I broke down crying as I finally told her the truth.

After sobbing for a few minutes, I reached out and wanted to hug her, but she pushed me away. She first said I was making it all up and I was mentally unstable. She said she had always been afraid I was mentally sick, and I would have to be treated for having delusions. I was shocked and hurt beyond words. I made her leave, and I told her not to come back.

She showed up once more a week later. There was a new hardness in her. She didn't bring me anything from home, and I wouldn't go anywhere with her to eat like we had done before. She started our visit by saying she had asked my Dad if I was telling the truth, and he admitted some of it was true. A little hope crept into my heart - she had come to ask forgiveness! She still loved me!

Instead, she crushed me completely by saying I had tempted him and caused him to sin. It was my fault he had lusted after me, and I should not have caused him to sin. She told me I was going to hell for what I had done and for bringing shame to our family.

There was nothing left in me. I didn't even feel

anger. In a way, I was not really surprised. It's probably the only way she can deal with it. I haven't seen her or talked to her since that day in September of 2000.

My Dad called once that I know of. He called on my birthday, October 8, a month after I left. At first, I wouldn't talk to him. Mack talked to him for a while before asking me if I was sure. I accepted the phone and sobbed while Dad tried one more time to get me to come home. He kept telling me it was my last chance for salvation and hope of heaven - I had to come back home and *"make it right."*

Finally, with Mack's support I was able to share with my Grandparents why I had left home and why I wasn't going back. My Grandparents tried not to take sides, but my parents demanded they choose - them or me. My Grandmother and my Dad had gone into a partnership to build a spec house, and they were right in the middle of selling it when all this happened. My Dad would only talk to her strictly about the business. Once that was finished, they stopped taking phone calls unless absolutely necessary and returned mailed letters unopened.

Dad and Mom both sent me a letter after that - I wouldn't talk to them on the phone anymore. Someone told me, years later, they shot and killed my dog Solomon when I refused to come home.

In the letters, they told me how great the family was now and all I had to do was come back home to make life perfect. It seems strange they could believe I would ever go back and pretend life was normal. I wasn't going back. Ever.

Everyone seemed to think I needed a counselor to

deal with my past. I completely disagreed but finally agreed to go, so everyone else would have some peace. I went for about a month but really wasn't getting any benefit. The counselor would listen to me for a while and then ask me how I felt about things. It seemed like a complete waste to me. I thought it was obvious that although I was devastated by the betrayal of my parents, I was blessed in many other ways and life would go on. For me, it was simply a matter of deciding I wasn't going to let the past seven years continue to weigh me down. I believe my past has helped me realize how blessed I am. I can certainly say there are many others who have experienced much greater hardships than I have.

We must choose our attitude! What motivates you, inspires you, and lifts you up? Get rid of the things that weigh you down by choosing to focus on what lifts you up.

Please note - I am not suggesting sexual abuse victims should not seek help or talk to someone. I encourage all victims to explore the available resources and seek professional help or counseling as needed. I continue to deal with some after effects, and I probably always will. I've learned to cope in my own way, but I am not advocating all victims do the same.

Check out the back of this book for some of the many resources available for victims of abuse, assault, or sexual trauma. Everyone deals with trauma differently. Some experience severe stress, fear, anxiety, anger, post-traumatic stress disorder (PTSD), guilt, and depression. Some may feel the need to turn to drugs or alcohol as a way to cope. Some may develop an identity disorder or eating disorder. There may be flashbacks or feelings of suicide.

Victims of abuse, rape, incest, or assault will need to develop a healthy coping mechanism to rebuild self-esteem and learn to heal. Talking to someone who is experienced in helping survivors overcome their experience in healthy ways can help guide you through the normal emotions and offer many resources to help you deal with the experience. Victims of sexual assault are more likely to suffer depression, post-traumatic stress disorder, abuse drugs or alcohol, or contemplate suicide.

It's important to take care of yourself emotionally and also physically. Self-care is difficult for many people and can be very challenging for a survivor. Make sure to take a balanced approach to a healthy lifestyle – healthy diet, adequate exercise, and plenty of sleep are basics for health and well-being for all of us and are especially important for someone experiencing emotional stress. **Counseling and emergency or crisis support is available.**

If someone you love is a victim, you may have emotions that you need help with as well. You may be shocked, and you may not know how to respond. You may experience anger, frustration, conflict, sadness, or fear. You must take care of yourself in order to be supportive of your loved one. Talk to a counselor or seek professional help if your feelings are overwhelming.

I believe a lot of the reason victims don't want to talk about their abuse is because they know their loved ones will be affected. Sometimes, the victim has learned to cope, but a close friend or family member doesn't know how to deal with it themselves or how to relate to the victim afterward. A victim may fear sharing a past abuse experience with a spouse because it may negatively impact their relationship. If your loved one has been a victim, it's very important you are supportive and non-judgmental. Make sure they know you care about them above all else. Encourage them to seek help. But remember, showing them you still love them and not blaming them is most important.

Statistics are shocking and tragic – there are an estimated 237,868 victims of sexual assault each year. One out of six American women, and one out of 33 American men have been the victim of an attempted or completed rape. An estimated 60% never get reported. (Source: www.rainn.org/statistics retrieved November 10, 2014)

From Ashes To Beauty

6

A NEW BEGINNING

Live in a constant state of gratitude, and laugh whenever possible. You will have days in which life seems to drop one load of bricks after another on you. The best way to escape that pile is to rise above it. Gratitude and good humor are the great elevators of life.

Nick Vujicic

His son Eric was 9 years old when I moved in with Mack. Eric had been through the divorce of his parents four years before, and then, Mack had remarried when Eric was about 7. That didn't work out, and Mack had just recently divorced again several months before we met in June. I don't know the details because I wasn't there, but I do know young Eric was a little skeptical of another stepmother, even though we had spent a little time together over the summer. Mack and I spent a lot of time making sure he felt included anytime he was around. Our weekends with Eric became the "fun" weekends, where we splurged a little bit. I was 11 years older than Eric and 11 years younger than Mack. Right in between the two of them, we had an interesting little family. Eric and I had fun!

I realized he didn't need another mother, and I didn't try to take her place. I focused on having fun with him, playing games, going to the movies when Mack worked late, and taking him out to eat. I ate more McDonald's meals than I might have eaten otherwise, but I knew it was about spending time with him and not about the food. I learned to throw a football. Not very well, but at least good enough to pass it to him, so he could throw it back. I wasn't perfect, but I gave it my best shot. It wasn't too bad for a young 19 year old who suddenly became a stepmother. I didn't realize then was that I was living out a leadership principle of building a relationship rather than trying to dictate from authority.

I had been living at Mack's house for almost a month. Things had settled into a routine. I had cleaned the place obsessively and immediately started taking over the cooking, grocery shopping, and even picking up Eric from school. But soon, I realized I wanted to be self-sufficient. Mack was wonderful, very supportive, and encouraged me to take my time in making any decisions. Because I had been dependent on someone for so long, my new freedom was incredible. I was determined I would become independent.

One of my friends had been boarding her horse at my parent's house. When I told her I had left home, she went to pick her horse up. I asked her to get my mare,

Cheyenne too. She was glad to help. We ended up stabling both horses at a local boarding stable in town close to where Mack and I lived. I was depending on Mack not only for my own living expenses, but also for my horse as well. It was clear - I needed a job.

I had to get proactive about life. Being proactive means responding based on values - taking initiative about your situation and doing something to improve it. Stephen R. Covey wrote about being proactive in his book, *The 7 Habits of Highly Effective People*. This is a powerful concept everyone should embrace and apply. Being proactive means responding based on your values rather than your feelings. Covey talks about the power of the "*pause between stimulus and response.*" We all have the ability to choose our response to any stimulus. Wow - that is POWERFUL stuff! If we are proactive, we will take initiative to act in life rather than wait to be acted upon. Proactive is the opposite of being reactive.

Covey teaches us, "*A serious problem with reactive language is that it becomes a self-fulfilling prophecy. People become reinforced in the paradigm that they are determined, and they produce evidence to support the belief. They feel increasingly victimized and out of control, not in charge of their life or their destiny. They blame outside forces – other people, circumstances, even the stars – for their own situation.*"

I have worked hard to be proactive through the years. Every single day. I wake up and think about how I am blessed and how I will be proactive in life. Writing this book is a choice to be proactive and respond based on the fact that I value how I can help someone else, rather than avoiding the emotions writing this book will cause.

I wasn't sure how someone would go about finding a job. Mack had a couple of suggestions, and I tried a few of them. I picked up a newspaper and looked through the employment ads. I went to the employment agency and took a typing test, passing with flying colors at 55 words per minute. I applied for a job as a clerk in a store that would be opening soon. All of that took about three hours, but I still didn't have a job. I was driving around, thinking about what I could do to earn money. I drove past a pizza restaurant, and the sign said "Now hiring." That was perfect! I knew I could wait tables.

I walked in and completed the two page application. I was interviewed on the spot. Susan was the store manager.

"You seem really mature for your age." She told me. *"But, that means I'm going to lean on you to help keep the kids around here in shape!"*

I laughed and agreed. *"I can do that. Just give me a shot."*

Susan hired me immediately and gave me two shirts. I was told to report to work the following day. I just about danced home. I was employed! I wouldn't have to ask someone permission to spend my money. I wouldn't have to ask Mack to give me money for groceries anymore.

Mack was excited for me although he seemed a little surprised at how fast I had found something. I showed up at work the next day and was shown how to set up for the lunch buffet. They opened at 11:00 a.m., and it only took five minutes before the first customer arrived. I was instructed to follow the manager for the first table and watch. After that, it was all mine. Talk about on the job training! I enjoyed serving and really found that most of the customers were nice. The lunch shift was pretty easy most of the time since there was a pizza buffet. All I had to do was get drinks and keep them filled. Then, bus the table afterward. For two hours, it would be busy, and I would run like crazy to keep up. Then, it would slow down, and I could catch up.

We only had one manager and one server most of the time, so I had to keep up with the entire restaurant. The manager was also the cook, and we both answered the phones. I learned valuable lessons about working with people there. I also learned that how people treat a waiter or waitress tells you a lot about their character.

My first shift went by fast, and I made $30.00 in tips. That might not seem like a lot to some people, but it was the first time I felt like I truly worked and earned something. I couldn't wait to buy groceries with my very own money. I drove home and was surprised Mack wasn't there. He had picked up Eric from school that day since I was at work, but neither of them were home. I called his cell, but he didn't answer. A little worried, I finally called his Mom, Joanne, but she didn't know where he was either. Really worried now, I tried to keep from feeling desperate. I was glad when he finally came home. I asked where he had been, but he just said "*Out shopping.*"

I put it out of my mind. Then, Mack told me to get dressed up. We were going to go out to eat to celebrate. My birthday was in three days, but we were going to eat out tonight. Always excited to get out of the house, I quickly changed from my work uniform. He took me to a nice restaurant in town at a nice hotel. I ordered pasta with shrimp, but I was a little put off because the shrimp came with the heads still attached! We were all the way to the key lime pie, and Mack was still a little reserved. He had been pretty quiet all night. I knew something was wrong. He picked up the little mint sprig from my pie plate and started fiddling with it. He said, "*I know you are pretty young, and you've been through a lot. Are you really serious about staying with me?*"

"*Of course I am, I wouldn't be here if I wasn't.*" I replied.

"*I know you believe in marriage, but I think we need to wait awhile to make sure you are making the right decision for you.*"

"*I know I've made the right decision for me. I don't have to wait for that.*"

He twisted the mint sprig into a circle. "*Are you sure? If this was a real ring, would you wear it?*" he asked.

"*Yes, I would. You know I want us to be married and not just living together.*" I replied. I took a sip of water, still not sure where he was going with this conversation but hoping he wasn't trying to break up with me. I looked back at him. He smiled.

In his hand, the mint sprig had suddenly turned into a diamond engagement ring!

I couldn't wait to share the news with my grandparents. I called them that night. Looking back now, I know everyone was worried about me, but I was not listening to a single word anyone said about "*slow down*" or "*maybe you should take some time.*" There are times in life where you know it's right. This was one of those times. To this day, I remain convinced God brought Mack to my life for a reason. He was agnostic at that time. While I knew it would be difficult to be joined to someone who didn't share my spiritual convictions, I held firmly to I Corinthians 7:14.

We spent New Year's Eve ringing in 2001 by planning our wedding. Eric, my soon to be stepson, would be the best man. We wanted a small wedding. I had heard about an old historic mansion in town that was perfect. We set the date for October.

Mack and I were married on October 27, 2001. We were blessed with friends and family around us as we said our vows. We went on a cruise for our honeymoon. We both love to travel to new places and have been blessed to be able to do that frequently in our years together. I had fun planning the wedding and kept it simple. My grandfather agreed to marry us, my other grandfather filmed the event for us, my grandmother went shopping with me for my dress, and my aunt agreed to sing at the wedding.

We didn't spend a lot of money, but it was a beautiful day just the same. The only thing that kept it from being a perfect day was the worry I had that my parents would show up and make a scene. They weren't invited of course. I don't even know if they knew exactly when and where the wedding was, but I still had a little fear they would show up and ruin my day. It didn't happen and the minor things that go wrong in big events didn't even bother me. I couldn't wait to change my name and get on with life.

One thing I have always known is I received the most amazing gift in the form of a husband who loves me. Although some would have considered us "unequally yoked" because Mack was agnostic when we married, I knew deep down my life would validate my faith, and certainly, Mack would be able to see through my faith the power of God. I was hopeful one day he would come to Christ because he would be able to see Christ living through me.

I stepped into the role of stepmother, determined to be the best stepmother I could be. I attended PTA meetings, helped with school events, booster club, and attended every one of Eric's baseball, football, track meets, and basketball games that I could possibly attend.

I learned to pack school lunches before leaving for work until Eric got to the age where it wasn't cool to take a home lunch. I enjoyed activities like school shopping and taking him shopping for something for Father's Day. I was always determined we would have a hot meal for dinner too; I can laugh at myself now and how silly I was about things like that. I've learned to relax in the years since. I now know stressing over dinner doesn't determine how kids turn out when they are grown. What's important is they know you love them unconditionally.

I learned to throw a football, take lots of pictures, and cheer for each touchdown or basket scored. Being a stepmother taught me a lot of important things. Looking back, it is easy to see the mistakes I made. But, I did the best I could at the time. I learned not to get mad when a dish was broken or a homework assignment was forgotten until late the night before it was due. I learned to keep supplies on hand for last minute brownies for the school party, and I learned to sleep with one ear tuned for the front door until Eric came home on the weekends, late at night.

If nothing else, I think children teach us we aren't

perfect, and we shouldn't expect them to be either. The earlier we learn that lesson, the better off in life we will be.

7

LIVE, LOVE, LAUGH, LEARN

There are no secrets to success. It is the result of preparation, hard work, and learning from failure.

Colin Powell

After we were married, it was time to get serious about a better job. I had been promoted to a shift manager at the pizza restaurant after just a few months there. I realized my future would be limited if I stayed there. I turned down the offer for Assistant Store Manager because I knew it would be nights and weekend work. Mack and I had agreed early on a schedule like that wasn't best for our family.

I started reading and getting ready to take my GED, which I passed the first time around. I applied for classes at the local community college and was accepted. I would be going to school two nights a week and taking three classes. I started looking hard for another job and found one as an office assistant at a small company that rebuilt small motors. It sounded great, good hours and right down the street from where Mack worked. It was less money than I was making as a shift manager at the pizza place, but I knew I had to get some office experience somewhere. I took the job.

Suddenly, life got a lot more complicated balancing a full time job and classes at least two nights a week, plus homework.

I had been working at that job for about six weeks when one of the owners came in and told us they were hiring a new man for the shop floor. He had just gotten out of prison, but they didn't think it would be a problem. I was one of two women who worked there, the rest were all men, and the owners were strict about not allowing us to be alone in the building or on the shop floor alone. I came home from work that day and shared with Mack the details on the new hire. He acted surprised and questioned me closely about the guy's name. When I told him, he was really upset. I asked why. He told me the man had just been released from prison after serving time following his conviction of raping a twelve-year-old girl. That upset me pretty bad too. We needed the money, I had already taken a pay cut to take this job, and I didn't want to go backward. But, I wasn't going back to work there. The next morning, I called in and said I wouldn't be coming back to work there. It's the only job I left without working out a notice.

I had still been doing some extra shift work waiting tables, and my manager was willing to give me a few extra shifts. I picked up a few extra days, but I was determined I wasn't going back to work there full time. I spent my day off the next week searching through the paper and applying for jobs. I wanted to be in the medical field or healthcare field and had thought one day I might go to nursing school, but I wasn't able to do that yet. I had to find a job fast or go back to waiting tables full time.

I looked up a temporary employment agency and walked in to apply. I was surprised they took my application right away and sent me over for a job interview the next day at a doctor's office. It was a receptionist type job, but it was a step in the right direction! I was offered the position; it was a temporary opening while one employee, Jennifer, was on maternity leave. I was able to spend two weeks training with her before she had the baby. I paid attention and learned really fast, so I was feeling okay by the time I had my first day on the job by myself. Praying it would turn into a permanent position, I worked very hard to learn everything quickly and make sure I made a good impression.

One day, a mother brought in her two children for appointments. The little boy was not feeling well, so she hurried him out of the exam room, looking for the bathroom. I told them it was down the hall - they didn't make it. The little boy got sick right before they got to the bathroom. My co-worker and I looked at each other. There was vomit all over the carpet. It obviously couldn't stay there. She just turned away. *"I can't do it, I'll get sick myself."* She told me. She apologized but wasn't able to help. I was desperate to make a good impression, so I cleaned it up, which was certainly not what I had in mind when I thought I wanted to work in a doctor's office! It paid off because when Jennifer decided not to return from maternity leave, I was hired.

If you work hard and give more than what you are required to do at work, it is easy to stand out as above average. It has always been important to me to work as hard as I would expect my team to work.

The next year, Mack and I worked very hard to pay off some bills. There were bills from his divorce, and we also had my school to pay for. I didn't want to be a burden on our finances. Plus, we bought a car for me to drive. That meant an extra car payment. We knew we wanted to buy a house, so we had to get our finances in good order. Mack worked a lot of overtime for the extra money, and we didn't spend much on extra stuff. About once a month or every few weeks, we would order wings and have them delivered. It was always a treat. We didn't really eat out or go anywhere during that time.

I got a monthly bonus from work but only if I didn't miss more than eight hours during the month, so that was another reason to work every day. The bonus was good. It could be up to $400 extra each month. I worked hard to learn everything I could at the office. When the opportunity came to attend a one-day optometry technician class, I jumped at the chance. I became a lot more knowledgeable. When the other office employee moved away, I was suddenly the senior employee working in the office. I took initiative to organize the office and set up a system to ensure all the insurance claims were filed and paid. I also started to track inventory and sales on the eyeglass frames to see which ones were selling, so I would know which ones to order.

Since sales affected my monthly bonus, I started thinking about how to make sure we met the goal each month.

What I didn't know was that experience was also teaching me how to think critically and solve problems. It was invaluable in helping me learn to deal with people. That, plus my time waiting tables, helped me learn a lot about people and interacting with them. I kept the part time job at the restaurant for a while because the extra money was good. Mack eventually talked me out of it because we weren't spending much time together between both of us working and both of us in school.

We bought a new house in June, 2003. We stayed the night for the first time the day we closed on the house – we didn't even have all of our furniture. We watched TV that night and ate fried chicken while sitting on the floor in the living room. We were happy though – it was a big purchase but perfect for us and really represented some stability for me. It felt weird signing all that paperwork. 30 years seemed like a long time to a 22 year old.

We settled in the house quickly. Money was tight because we were now making a large house payment. We still had fun, and it was a far cry from sitting out behind our old mobile home in a lawn chair under the sprinkler. I wasn't making a lot at the doctor's office even with the monthly bonus. I had hoped for some opportunity there but obviously wasn't going to get more than a minimal raise from time to time.

I started looking for another job. I wasn't yet qualified for much, but I knew a bigger physician practice would surely have more opportunity and possibly pay more. I took a day off from work and spent most of it dropping off resumes at local places. I knew sometimes walking in and talking to people helped make a really good impression and guaranteed my resume made it to the front desk at least, in case they were actively looking. One thing was for sure – I had gone as far as I could at the job where I was.

It paid off – I got a job interview within a few weeks at a physician practice. The office manager there was married to someone I knew. While I didn't know her personally, I knew of her. The interview went really well.

She offered me a front desk position at slightly more than I was making already, but I knew the opportunities would be much better. This was a bigger physician office, and they had a corporate office as well. The first day there was crazy – the phone seemed to ring every 30 seconds. It was my job to answer it, check in patients, process paperwork, verify insurance, make copies, and anything else that popped up. I learned really quickly. Every time the phone rang, I made it my mission to answer within one ring if possible. One of the physicians even commented on how quickly and professionally I answered the phone.

Things were looking good; I was making a really good impression and didn't mind the fast pace of the office because the day flew by. Once again, I was dealing with people almost constantly and quickly learned how I acted toward patients made all the difference in their attitude towards me. I was also learning a lot about insurance and medical coding. All the hours I had spent on the computer as a teenager started to pay off as I learned about new software systems. Within a few months, a position opened up as a medical assistant. I applied. My manager told me she was hesitant to promote me because she didn't want to lose me at the front desk!

I worked hard. Although I was only able to take a few classes each semester, I was enjoying learning and school in general. Some subjects were more interesting than others, but this was the first time I had been exposed to a formal learning environment. Overall, it seemed pretty easy. The teachers told me what material to learn; all I had to do was learn it. The days were hard and long - I would work all day, and then, either go to school or go do homework.

If we give up easily in life, we won't be able to accomplish much. I have never been a great runner - I'm not a natural runner. But, I have completed several marathons because I figured out running a marathon was 80% mental and 20% physical. As long as you are healthy and not injured, it's a matter of sheer determination to keep running for 26.2 miles. I applied the same concept to get through nearly 10 years of going to college at night and working during the day. Being persistent and moving forward a little bit every day will help you accomplish your goals. The key is to keep moving. Don't let anyone or anything hold you back from reaching your goal.

I picked up a second job as a waitress at a steak house in the fall of 2006. At that point, I was working seven days a week and going to school full time. I was working one Saturday night when the restaurant was busy, and I got a table with a big group of people. Since it was Saturday, the kitchen was running behind. I was anxiously waiting on the appetizers. As soon as they came up, I grabbed the appetizers and plates. I had to carry the food on a big tray.

In fact, when I trained as a server, I had to learn to carry the tray on my shoulder – it's much harder than it looks. You start out by carrying a tray full of salads in case you drop it.

I loaded up the tray that night and hefted it to my shoulder. I grabbed the tray jack as I practically ran out of the kitchen. I walked through the restaurant towards my table.

I almost made it. I was about 10 feet from my table when I stepped on my shoelace. Down came the tray full of appetizers and plates. The bowl of ranch dressing came down right on the front of my shirt!! I ended up in a pile of ranch dressing and broken appetizer plates.

Right then and there, I had a choice. That could be the worst waitressing moment of my life. Or, it could be the best. Life is all about how we choose to take it. I learned to laugh at myself that night, and I learned to double knot my shoelaces.

It took five years, but I finally graduated in 2007 from the Community College with an Associate's degree in Office Management and Medical Coding. I took the entire summer of 2007 off from school, and I only worked one job which was a nice break.

By the fall of 2007 however, I was considering going back to school. I had received a promotion to Office Manager but was expected to continue my duties as a medical assistant as well. Since I was filling two jobs, I started having to put in long hours. It wasn't unusual to put in a 60-hour workweek on a salary meant for a 40-

hour workweek. I certainly made a lot of mistakes as a manager, but I learned a lot too.

I checked my options and decided I would take a few core classes to be eligible for enrollment to an accelerated Bachelor program from Faulkner University. I needed a few core classes and requested permission to be off on Monday afternoons in order to attend school. I was working at least 60 hours a week and was shocked when my request was denied. I was doing the work of two full time employees and wasn't going to be allowed to leave a few hours early one day a week to attend a biology class that wasn't offered any other time. Tension was high at the office too as I tried new methods to improve efficiency only to run into the roadblock of people who didn't like change.

Now, I realize my leadership skills weren't developing as fast as my technical skills. That caused conflict. At the time however, all I knew was every time I tried to make things better for my team at work it ended up in a mess. One afternoon, I butted heads with a doctor as I tried to improve the workflow at the front desk. It ended up in a stalemate. I locked myself in the office and cried from the stress. I went home that night knowing it was time to find another job. There was a never-ending tug of war, and I was in the middle between the physicians and the administration at the corporate office.

I was hired into the compliance department at a local community hospital in January 2008. Life became better overnight. I went from working 60 plus hour workweeks to a regular workweek with normal work hours, more flexibility, better benefits, and a terrific boss whom I adored. I spent the large majority of the first eight weeks learning new skills and wrapping my arms around the detailed world of healthcare licensing and regulations.

Life was going great until one day my director announced she was going to step down and just work part time. *"What's next?"* was a question I kept asking. I was more than a little nervous – I was a new employee at the organization, and I didn't want to suddenly be working for someone else with no say in the matter. My department was merged with another department. I was given some slightly new responsibilities and two additional supervisors to report to. That was a challenge for me but certainly taught me how to balance competing projects and priorities.

Robin Sharma said, *"Hard work opens doors and shows the world that you are serious about being one of those rare – and special – human beings who use the fullness of their talents to do their very best."*

I was determined to advance in the organization. In one year, I was promoted to head of my department when a position opened up. The values of the organization fit me very well, and I thought I would work there until I retired. It felt like an extended family. I was blessed with opportunities to grow. I went back to school on a scholarship program and graduated with my undergrad and then graduate degree within three years, through accelerated executive programs at Faulkner University and AUM, finishing both programs with a 4.0 GPA.

I took advantage of several leadership development courses that were offered as well. I jumped at the chance to learn anything and everything I could and still felt something was missing. I was busy – no doubt about that and certainly growing professionally, but my personal development was slow because all my effort was focused on growing my skills rather than developing my character.

I found a passion for teaching group fitness and was certified to teach in early 2009, the same time I went back to school. Teaching classes at the gym was a great way to ensure I was working out regularly, and I loved connecting with the people.

8

THE NEXT CHAPTER

Open your eyes, look within. Are you satisfied with the life you've been living?

Bob Marley

It's the little things that make a difference in our results...reading every day helps us grow. Exercising every day helps us stay healthy. Eating right every day helps us maintain a healthy weight. We first must establish our priorities. Then plan life around those things that are valuable to us. I always tell people you can tell what is important to someone by how they spend their time and money.

Exercise is an important priority for me because it helps me maintain balance in my life, stay fit, and stay healthy. Six days a week, I exercise before I do anything else - first thing in the morning. That way, nothing comes up that will prevent me from getting my workout in. If something is a priority, that is where I should focus my time and energy first. Then, other tasks can be done.

Think about the difference one small choice or decision can make over time:

"Water boils at 212 degrees, but at 211 degrees, it is still just hot water. One extra degree, an increase of less than one-half of one percent, can make the difference between a pot of languishing liquid and a bubbling caldron of power." John C. Maxwell

Less than one-half of one percent! Talk about the power of small – small things can be big things if they are in the right place at the right time. Think about all the little things we do in our day to day lives – they don't always seem to matter. But collectively, they add up to something huge. To me, this is why we have to be intentional in planning our priorities and lives each and every day. Daily discipline can add up to something powerful over time.

After exercise, I plan my day around other priorities. This helps me make sure I get what is important done. A plan also helps me stay organized – as I look ahead to what my day holds I can better prepare. Using an effective calendar system is one tool I find invaluable in my life. We all have some examples of systems in our life that work. Maybe you have a certain place you always put your car keys, so you always know where to find them. But, if for some reason they aren't there, you waste valuable time looking for them. I use many different systems to make the most efficient use of my time.

It's important to establish our priorities based on what we value. I seldom watch TV. It's not something that will take me in the direction I want to go. It certainly has its place for relaxation - I'm not saying all TV is bad. It can be relaxing, entertaining, or educational. But, it's nothing I am willing to spend my precious time on very often. Reading a book brings me more value than watching TV shows. What you choose to spend your time on will determine what direction you go in - forward or backward.

One morning at the gym, we had an entire ROTC class come in and take a group fitness class. There were about 50 people, mostly young men, who came in and thought it was going to be a piece of cake to take this class. I certainly don't look intimidating. I was very clear about how much weight I recommended they put on their bar to start with, so they would be able to finish.

Unfortunately, some of them didn't listen to my recommendations and loaded up their bars with as much weight as I had. That was a lesson in humility for some of them as they struggled to make it to the end of the first big track! Group fitness classes might sound easy. But, let me tell you, it can be a great way to get in shape because the workout is more about endurance than heavy weights.

In May 2012, I graduated Phi Kappa Phi with my MBA. For the first time in 10 years, I considered myself finished with school. What's next? I asked myself.

Mack and I enjoyed mountain biking. We raced the state series in Alabama and Georgia in 2011. I took the champion jersey in my division for both states. We moved up to a more competitive division for 2012. I was excited when I won the championship in both states at this level too. I had discovered my competitive nature within and vigorously applied myself to a training schedule focused on physically performing the best I could.

We had also become involved in forming a local mountain bike chapter. I took on the role of grant writer and secretary for the organization. We helped get 15 miles of multi-purpose trails built in our local state park and committed many hours to volunteer work, trail work, leading group rides, and developing the sport in our area. I was dreaming of racing at the national level when life took a new turn unexpectedly. John Lennon said it well, *"Life is what happens while you are busy making other plans."*

Mack decided to attend a conference in Florida one weekend in June 2012. I didn't go because I couldn't take the day off work, so he and Eric went. He gave me a call at the end of the first day. He was so excited he couldn't talk clearly. *"I just found out John Maxwell has a team, and I can join it for $5,000. This is perfect for me and my business and will help me write my own book!"*

I wasn't quite as enthusiastic. *"You spent how much? What exactly do you get?"* I asked, a little worried this was not a sound investment, at best.

"Well, you get access to teach and train on John's books!" He excitedly shared a little more before dropping another bomb on me. *"Oh, I signed up Eric too. At $5,000, this is a BARGAIN!"*

"Um. Ok. What's next?" I asked, while mentally trying to decide what else we could have done with so much money. *"We will come back in August and get certified!"* He

was so excited, I couldn't help but be happy for him. I was glad he and Eric were able to take a few extra days at the end of their trip vacationing in Florida.

What I didn't expect was how he started to grow afterward. While I have always been an avid reader, Mack has never really been interested in reading and now suddenly he was ordering books, highlighting quotes, and building a new website for his business. I felt a little overwhelmed, but when he offered the chance for me to join the program the following February, I agreed. By this time, my job at the hospital had turned into a position with a lot more responsibility, several additional team members, and much longer workdays. I was working once again six and seven days a week, especially when Mack was traveling for work. I no longer had schoolwork. I had simply transferred that extra time and energy into my job.

Mack and I took a wonderful mountain biking vacation in October 2012. We spent two weeks driving to New Mexico, Colorado, Utah, Texas, Arkansas, Oklahoma and back to Alabama, stopping along the way to mountain bike. There was a lot of time in the car, but I think it was the best trip we have ever been on, except our vacations with Eric. We rode Slick Rock, one of the most technical mountain biking trails in the U.S. It took almost three hours. I was exhausted by the time we finished but proud I did it. I had come a long way from the girl who wouldn't ride off a curb along the sidewalk.

Aa few months later, in February 2013, I attended the John Maxwell Leadership Certification. Life changed quickly, and I started a new chapter in my life when I resigned from the hospital at the beginning of 2014.

I've never looked back with regret. Sometimes, I am asked if I miss working at the hospital. I always answer, *"I miss the people there, but I found a calling instead of a career. I wouldn't go back."*

For me, the feeling of living in God's purpose for my life is beyond compare and no amount of money would cause me to change that. I am truly blessed.

After sharing my one-minute presentation at the Les Brown speaker training event on August 14, 2013, I walked off the stage and to the back of the room, numb. I had opened up my soul and became vulnerable in sharing something that had defined me for years. What I had found was the strength to share and realized while the experiences of my past would not define me – it was up to me to decide how it would refine me. I could have continued to live as a victim. Instead, I choose to live in God's purpose by overcoming my circumstances. There had been a six-month struggle within as I decide whether I should tell my story.

After six months of trying to tell God what I wanted to do, I finally stopped and listened.

I had to overcome the fear of sharing my past. I knew that would change the way people looked at me and that scared me. I was afraid people would look at me different – and they do. As humans, we all bring our own paradigm to the way we see things. We bring our own experiences and our own stories with us. That affects how we see the world.

10 days after returning from the Les Brown event, I asked to meet with my boss. I cried as I shared I was going to resign my job and pursue my calling in speaking and writing. I knew that God had opened a door for me,

and I had to step through it right then or live the rest of my life regretting it. Even more difficult than telling her was telling my team. I felt like I was letting them down in a way, but I knew I could no longer ignore the feeling there was more for me to accomplish outside the hospital.

9

ACHIEVE ABUNDANT LIFE

When I stand before God at the end of my life, I would hope that I would not have a single bit of talent left, and could say, 'I used everything you gave me'.

Erma Bombeck

Whatever we decide to do with our lives, we will only be average if we aren't living with passion and purpose. When you discover what you are passionate about and when you discover your purpose, that is where you will find the energy to excel. You will find it easy to work longer hours or practice over and over because it's something you are passionate about and something you enjoy.

One thing is absolutely certain – life is too short and too precious to spend it working in a job where you are unhappy. We are all given 24 hours in a day, and we can spend them any way we choose – but we only get to spend them once. It's as important to spend our time on our purpose and our passion as it is to stop spending time in the wrong areas.

Saying "no" can be a most effective tool in finding balance and harmony in life and allows us to focus time on the important areas, so we can spend our time on our purpose. I struggle with saying "no" sometimes because I love to help people. It's really difficult for me to tell someone "no" if I feel like I can possibly manage to fit whatever I'm being asked to do into my schedule. I realize however, if I never said "no," I would not have time for the things that allow me to live my purpose.

Aligning your activities with your purpose will be difficult if you haven't yet discovered your purpose. Often, it is a journey. As we grow and develop, we are better able to focus more specifically on purpose. If we are in alignment with our purpose, it will be easy to set goals.

It's important to know our strengths and our weaknesses when we consider living in our purpose. John Maxwell said it very well, "*People's purpose in life is always connected to their area of giftedness.*" If you aren't working where you are talented, you may work extremely hard without achieving great results. Focus the same energy toward an area where you are talented, and you will achieve excellence.

Sometimes, the key to our passion can be found in our hobbies because that is where we spend our free time. What do you love to do so much that you dream about doing it all the time? What do you love to do so much that you would lose sleep to do it? Sometimes, we need to ask ourselves if a part time hobby has a bigger place in our life. What do you do so well other people would pay you to do it? Where is the sweet spot where your passion and purpose overlap? Find that, and you are well on your way.

What makes me different than those who have not been able to overcome their past? What was it about me compared to someone else who turned to prostitution, drugs, alcohol, or suicide? What has helped me to not only overcome and survive what I went through but also to thrive, and "Achieve Abundant Life?" How have I been able to find purpose in the pain? What can I share with others to help them also overcome their own circumstances?

Our past experiences and past choices made us who we are today. But, our choices today will define us tomorrow. How we handle what life gives us will determine if it makes us stronger and better or not. There are many examples of people who have been able to overcome their circumstances and use their experience to help inspire someone else. Many of these inspirational people have helped me by reminding me of the power of positive attitude.

People who overcame insurmountable obstacles and now make a difference in the lives of other people inspire me: Nick Vujicic, Bethany Hamilton, Liz Murray, Viktor Frankl, and Les Brown. Also, people who aren't famous but live out these principles every day and quietly make a difference in the lives of someone else inspire me. Look around you. You can find examples of people who have successfully applied personal leadership lessons to their lives. You too can apply these principles and Achieve Abundant Life.

I've talked about these principles throughout this book and in summary, here are the principles I have applied to my life:

1) Be PROACTIVE and PERSISTENT
2) Have PRIORITIES and a PLAN
3) Practice PERSONAL and PROFESSIONAL GROWTH
4) Find your PASSION and PURPOSE

If you aren't happy with where you are in life, what are you doing about it? If you are dissatisfied with your circumstances, then be willing to do the work to improve yourself. We must grow relative to both character and competency in order to change things in our lives. That means getting comfortable being uncomfortable.

Learning to mountain bike was one thing that helped me get outside of my comfort zone and grow because it taught me so much more than how to ride a bike. Neale Donald Walsh said, "*Life begins at the end of your comfort zone.*" Life might or might not begin at the end of the comfort zone, but growth certainly begins there.

I think about when I learned to drive. When I was four years old, I didn't know what I didn't know about driving a car. I was completely unaware of that skill. At age 14, I was aware I didn't know how to drive, but I still didn't know how to do it. I was still in the comfort zone when it came to driving a car. When I started learning to drive at age 15, I became pretty uncomfortable!

There were three pedals, and I only had two feet! I had to watch the speedometer, the rearview mirror, the two lines in front of me, and figure out which pedal to push, all at the same time. That is when I was learning the new skill - growth in life occurs when we get outside of our comfort zone. Now, I can't tell you how many times I've driven home and don't remember the drive. I'm back in my comfort zone when it comes to driving a car, and I'm not learning anything because I've already mastered that task.

Our personal, professional, and spiritual growth happens outside the comfort zone too. We must be intentional about it because it's uncomfortable, and we won't automatically embrace it. It is more important to grow our character and develop our personal growth than our competency and professional growth. Our character and integrity is critical to success in relationships at work or at home. Trust is the key element of integrity - we must build trust with the people in our lives by demonstrating integrity.

Trust. It's something so precious in relationships. Stephen M. R. Covey calls it, "The One Thing That Changes Everything" in his book, The Speed of Trust. He states, "Violations of integrity are the most difficult of all to restore in all relationships, whether they are personal, family, professional, organizational, or in the marketplace."

Choosing to extend trust to someone requires belief in them and confidence in who they say they are. It is a choice we make based on the actions, words, and behavior of the person. I've always believed in giving someone the benefit of the doubt - until there is no doubt. Then, there is no benefit. That doesn't mean trust cannot be rebuilt, over time, but it means I don't automatically extend it again and again when the person has demonstrated a lack of integrity. It does mean once trust is violated, it does take time, deliberate effort, and energy to work to restore the relationship. It can be done – and sometimes, the relationship can become stronger after trust has been restored. You can't rush the process, but you can follow it. Like everything truly worth having, trust doesn't cost us anything. Trust cannot be bought, but it can be developed over time.

Let me be clear here. – If you choose not to quickly extend trust again after it has been violated, that is entirely separate from forgiveness. Extending forgiveness is something we need to do to let go of any feelings of anger, blame, or vindictiveness. If someone breaks trust, there is an opportunity for us to grow in our ability to be a better person and forgive the wrong done. Sometimes, people ask me how I could possibly forgive my parents. I learned a long time ago that I needed to do that in order to move on with my life.

Forgiving another person is part of our own personal growth journey – we must choose to move forward down the path rather than backwards. Is there someone in your life you need to forgive? Is there something you need to let go of in order to move on?

10

HOPE AND HEALING

Healing doesn't mean the damage never existed. It means the damage no longer controls your life...

Akshay Dubey

I've moved on. Learning to let go was hard, but I refuse to feel like a victim the rest of my life. In truth, it's hard every day. There are moments that surprise me, when something hits me hard and unexpectedly. But, I choose to let it go. I've learned to laugh more, and I've learned to cry more. I've learned, to my sorrow, there are many more like me, women and men, with a story to tell that is so painfully close to mine. We all have something we must let go of before we can grasp what's ahead.

My way forward is a hopeful journey, and I am blessed to be traveling it. Life goes on – and so must I.

I have learned:

Life is precious.
I need to forgive.
Tears can heal.
I am not perfect and no one expects me to be.
Laughter is a gift from God.
I'm more blessed when I give than receive.
I must be humble, for I don't know what I don't know.
It's not about what I do, it's about who I am.
I can't buy love, happiness, friendship, trust, faith, health and hope.
Those things I can't buy are the most valuable.

I think the most important lesson I have learned is each day is an opportunity for us to use our time, energy, and God-given gifts for His glory and helping others. Each day is a clean sheet of paper. What we write on it is our decision.

What will you write on yours?

Ria as a baby (1981)

Ria at 15 years old (1995)

The house Ria grew up in

Mack and Ria's
Wedding (2001)

Ria and Cheyenne
(2002)

MBA Graduation
(2012)

Ria with Mack, after winning
her first mountain bike race
(2011)

Ria with John Maxwell
(2013)

Les Brown, Ria and Mack
(2013)

Ria with Nick Vujicic
(2014)

Ria speaking from the stage
(2014)

Ria teaching group fitness
(2014)

Excerpt from *ACHIEVE: Maximize Your Potential with 7 Keys to Success and Significance,*
By Ria Story

"Character is the ability to meet the demands of reality."
~ Henry Cloud

Integrity has four components: 1) Character; 2) Courage; 3) Commitment (to self); and 4) Congruency (with others).

Character is the foundational component because all the other components are built on top of character. In fact, integrity is determined by character. And, character is the determining success factor in life.

Your character and integrity determine how you will face life's challenges. Your response to success, failure, joy, pain, sickness, health, poverty, wealth, and the *"demands of reality"* will all be based upon your character.

Character is based upon intangible characteristics that will determine your success: attitude, work ethic, perseverance, resilience, discipline, courage, humility, and many more. Character is not based upon, or determined by, your education, background, race, ancestors, or experiences in life. Each and every day, you are writing your internal script by choosing your values. Then, your script (resulting character based upon the values you have internalized) will dictate your decisions and responses in any given situation.

Competency is your talent, natural gifts, skills, and abilities. Our character, not our competency, determines how far we will go and what we will ACHIEVE. Unfortunately, many people spend years developing their competency and little time developing their character and integrity.

In June 2013, I went to Guatemala on a mission trip. This wasn't a mission trip like you usually hear about where you take medical supplies and teach the Gospel. It was a mission trip to start the cultural transformation of Guatemala. This initiative had been years in the making because the President of Guatemala had asked John Maxwell for support in teaching the nation personal leadership principles.

While I was in Guatemala, our team trained various leaders; from Boy Scout troop leaders to top-level government officials. 150 coaches trained over 20,000 leaders in three days. One of the things we shared with them was 87% of who we are is determined by our character. The other 13% is what we know, our skills, knowledge and technical abilities. In other words, 87% of our success and influence comes from what we are, not what we know.

It's not always easy to live true to your values. Sometimes, having character requires you to face uncomfortable truths and stand up for what you believe. This happened to me early in my career.

I had recently been promoted to a new position in the organization where I worked. My new role was one of two identical positions in the organization. "Christy" (name changed) was my counterpart, and we had the same job duties and expectations. Christy had been there many years and had settled comfortably into her routine, so I knew I could learn from her.

I had a good work ethic, and I was eager to continue to make a good impression, hoping to continue moving up in the organization. Always a quick learner, I watched carefully how Christy did her job, and then I tried to see if I could make the process more efficient. I made some mistakes but quickly learned how to be more effective and efficient in my new role. And, I didn't mind working hard, taking initiative, and stepping up without being asked.

One day, my boss called me aside. *"Hey Ria,"* she said, *"Come here a moment."*

"Sure," I replied, *"What do you need?"*

"I've got a little problem," she chuckled, *"And, I need your help."* Always eager to help, I nodded for her to continue. *"Ok, sure."*

"Everyone has noticed how quick you are learning, and you are really doing an outstanding job."

"Thank you!" I smiled, excited she had noticed my efforts and hard work.

"But the problem is, you are making Christy look bad. She's been here a lot longer and you are causing some problems for her. There are some concerns about why she doesn't do as good a job as you are doing. And, people are asking me why I let her get away with slacking off."

I could feel my smile starting to melt. *"Oh?"*

"Can you just slow down sometimes and try not to be so fast at your work? I don't mean you have to screw up on purpose but maybe wait until someone asks you before you do something that needs to be done."

I couldn't believe it. My boss was telling me I needed to slack off because Christy didn't want to work hard.

I knew she and Christy were friends outside of work. They took trips together, went out for lunch, and even had drinks after work sometimes too. I also knew I wasn't going to slow down for one minute. I wasn't making Christy look bad, she was making me look good.

It put me in an uncomfortable position, but I told my boss I wasn't going to compromise my work ethic. And then, I showed her by continuing to work as hard as I could. Within two years, I had her job.

Character is having the right values. Integrity is living true to them. We must have the character to meet the demands of reality and the integrity to choose to do so.

Excerpt from *Straight Talk: The Power of Effective Communication,* by Ria Story

I was nearly 20 years old before I realized I liked people. I never considered myself to be an "introvert" although most people would have. I simply didn't talk to people. Ask me a question, and you would get a monosyllabic response that discouraged any further dialogue. It's not that I didn't want to talk or communicate with people – I simply didn't know how.

I grew up very isolated, living on a farm in the middle of the woods. I was homeschooled. We didn't attend church regularly, and my social contact growing up was mainly limited to field trips with other homeschoolers. In the early 1980's in Alabama, opportunities for homeschooled children to participate in extra-curricular activities were limited, and my parents didn't pursue most of them.

I was also sexually abused by my father from age 12 – 19. Growing up with feelings of shame, guilt, hurt, and unworthiness only compounded my natural tendency to be withdrawn, even after I left home at 19. I share more about my story in some of my other books, *Ria's Story From Ashes To Beauty* and *Beyond Bound and Broken: A Journey of Healing and Resilience.*

Leaving home without a job, a car, or even a high school diploma, I got a crash course on the need for communication in "normal" society.

At 19, I had a great education, ability to think critically, reasoning skills, proactive attitude, and willingness to work hard. What I didn't have was the critical ability to connect with other people and communicate *effectively*.

Since I didn't have a GED or a high school diploma, finding a way to make a living wasn't going to be easy, but I was determined to start making money and earning my way.

My first job was working as a server at a pizza restaurant. I worked the lunch shift, Monday through Friday every day, from 11:00 – 2:00. Most customers would have the all-you-can-eat pizza and salad buffet because it was fast and didn't cost too much.

I was the only lunch server for all 36 tables in the restaurant. My job was to set up the buffet, keep the salad bar stocked and clean, make the tea, fill the ice bin, stock the soda machine, answer the phone, take delivery orders, greet the customers when they entered, take and fill their drink orders, keep dirty plates bussed, refill their drinks, check them out at the cash register, clean the tables, chairs, and floor after the customer left, wash all the dishes, put them away, and restock everything before I left. All for $2.13 per hour, plus any tips I made.

The lunch buffet was $5.99, and a drink was $1.35. Most customer bills came to less than $8.00 for lunch. The average tip is 10% for a buffet, so the best tip I could expect would be about $1.00 – and that's if I hustled really hard to keep their soda refilled and the dirty plates bussed. If I was too busy and the customer ran out of tea, I may not have gotten a tip at all.

I learned quickly that being an "introverted" waitress wasn't going to work. If I didn't smile at the customers, they thought I was unfriendly. If I didn't greet them enthusiastically, they didn't feel welcome or appreciated. If I didn't remember the names of the regular customers and what they liked to drink, they often wouldn't even leave me the change from their dollar.

I learned a lot of things during my years of waiting tables, off and on earlier in my career. You see the best and the worst of people when you wait tables. But, the most important lesson I learned was to take initiative and connect with my customers. **Communicating information wasn't enough. I had to connect with them.** I could tell them where to get a plate and take their drink order, but how I did it made all the difference in whether they left me anything at all, or sometimes, several dollars.

What I want to share with you in this book are some of the lessons I've learned about connecting with people and communicating effectively. There aren't any shortcuts to success, but I hope I can help you avoid the detours and map out a faster route.

Effective communication skills are critical to our success in life.

On the professional side, the ability to communicate and relate to customers, co-workers, employees, or your boss can determine your career potential and define your success.

On the personal side, communication with your spouse, children, parents, and friends will determine your satisfaction in life (at least some of it) and define your relationships.

Regardless of your preferred personality style, or whether you consider yourself an introvert or extrovert, dealing with other people is a fact of life. Almost any situation you can think of requires you to come in contact and interact with other people sooner or later.

Your eye color cannot be changed. Your genetic ability to run a four-minute mile cannot be changed. Your ability to communicate CAN be changed. **Communication is a skill anyone can learn, and everyone can learn to do it better.**

ABOUT THE AUTHOR

Like many, Ria faced adversity in life. Ria was sexually abused by her father from age 12 - 19, forced to play the role of his wife, and even shared with other men. Desperate to escape, she left home at 19 without a job, a car, or even a high school diploma. Ria learned to be resilient, not only surviving, but thriving. She worked her way through college, earning her MBA with a cumulative 4.0 GPA, and had a successful career in the corporate world of administrative healthcare.

Ria's background includes more than 10 years in administrative healthcare with several years in leadership and management including working as the Director of Compliance for a large healthcare organization. Ria's responsibilities included oversight of thousands of organizational policies, organizational compliance with all State and Federal regulations, and responsibility for several million dollars in Medicare appeals.

Today, Ria is a motivational leadership speaker, TEDx Speaker, and author of 11 books, including Leadership Gems for Women. Ria is a certified leadership speaker and trainer and was selected three times to speak on stage at International John Maxwell Certification Events. Motivational speaker Les Brown also invited Ria to share the stage with him in Los Angeles, CA.

Ria has a passion for health and wellness and is a certified group fitness instructor. She has completed several marathons and half-marathons and won both the Alabama and Georgia Women's State Mountain Biking Championships in 2011 and 2012.

Ria shares powerful leadership principles and tools of transformation from her journey to equip and empower women, helping them maximize their potential in life and leadership.

ABOUT MACK STORY

Mack began his career in manufacturing on the front lines of a machine shop. He grew himself into upper management and found his niche in lean manufacturing and along with it, developed his passion for leadership.

With more than 20 years working with and on the front lines, he brings a powerful blend of practical experience and leadership knowledge to his clients. Mack is a published author of several leadership books including: Blue-Collar Leadership, Blue-Collar Leadership & Supervision, Defining Influence, 10 Values of High Impact Leaders, MAXIMIZE Your Potential, MAXIMIZE Your Leadership Potential, Change Happens, and more.

He understands that everything rises and falls on leadership.

For more detailed information on Mack, please visit TopStoryLeadership.com.

RESOURCES FOR RECOVERY

If you have experienced sexual assault or abuse or know of a loved one who has, there are resources available to help.

National Sexual Assault Hotline:
800-656-HOPE (4673)

Visit: www.centers.rainn.org to search for a local crisis center in your area.

Rape, Abuse, & Incest National Network has information and resources available on their website:
www.rainn.org

Department of Defense/Military Support:
www.safehelpline.org or 877-995-5247

National Sexual Violence Resource Center:
www.nsvrc.org

Order books online at Amazon or RiaStory.com

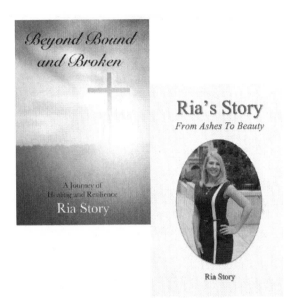

Ria Story

In *Beyond Bound and Broken,* Ria shares how she overcame the shame, fear, and doubt she developed after enduring years of extreme sexual abuse by her father. Forced to play the role of a wife and even shared with other men due to her father's perversions, Ria left home at 19 without a job, a car, or even a high-school diploma. This book also contains lessons on resilience and overcoming adversity that you can apply to your own life.

In *Ria's Story From Ashes To Beauty,* Ria tells her personal story of growing up as a victim of extreme sexual abuse from age 12 – 19, leaving home to escape, and her decision to tell her story

Order books online at Amazon or RiaStory.com

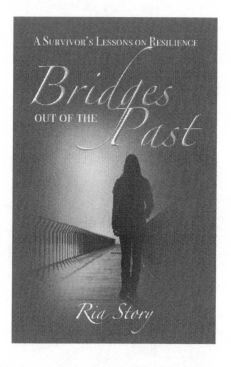

It's not what happens to you in life. It's who you become because of it. We all experience pain, grief, and loss in life. Resilience is the difference between *"I didn't die,"* and *"I learned to live again."* In this captivating book on resilience, Ria walks you through her own horrific story of more than seven years of sexual abuse by her father. She then shares how she learned not only to survive, but also to thrive in spite of her past. Learn how to overcome challenges, obstacles, and adversity in your own life by building a bridge out of the past and into the future.

(Watch 7 minutes of her story at RiaStory.com/TEDx)

Order books online at Amazon or RiaStory.com

Note: Leadership Gems is the generic, non-gender specific, version of Leadership Gems for Women. The content is very similar.

Women are naturally high impact leaders because they are relationship oriented. However, it's a *"man's world"* out there and natural ability isn't enough to help you be successful as a leader. You must be intentional.

Ria packed these books with 30 leadership gems which very successful people internalize and apply. Ria has combined her years of experience in leadership roles of different organizations along with years of studying, teaching, training, and speaking on leadership to give you these 30, short and simple, yet powerful and profound, lessons to help you become very successful, regardless of whether you are in a formal leadership position or not.

Order books online at Amazon or RiaStory.com

You have hopes, dreams, and goals you want to achieve. You have aspirations of leaving a legacy of significance. You have untapped potential waiting to be unleashed. But, unfortunately, how to maximize your potential isn't something addressed in job or skills training. And sadly, how to achieve success and find significance in life isn't something taught in school, college, or by most parents.

In *ACHIEVE: Maximize Your Potential with 7 Keys to Unlock Success and Significance*, Ria shares lessons to help you become more influential, more successful and maximize your potential in life. Three-page chapters are short, yet powerful, and provide principles on realizing your potential with actionable takeaways. These brief vignettes provide humorous, touching, or sad lessons straight from the heart that you can immediately apply to your own situation.

Order books online at Amazon or RiaStory.com

Become inspired by this 30-day collection of daily devotions for women, where you will find practical advice on intentionally living with a grateful heart, inspirational quotes, short journaling opportunities, and scripture from God's Word on practicing gratitude.

Order books online at Amazon or RiaStory.com

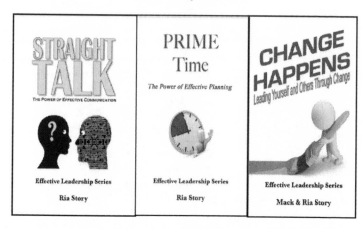

Ria's *Effective Leadership Series* books are written to develop and enhance your leadership skills, while also helping you increase your abilities in areas like communication and relationships, time management, planning and execution, leading and implementing change. Look for more books in the *Effective Leadership Series*:

- *Straight Talk: The Power of Effective Communication*

- *PRIME Time: The Power of Effective Planning*

- *Change Happens: Leading Yourself and Others through Change (Co-authored by Ria & Mack Story)*

- *Leadership Gems & Leadership Gems for Women*

Order books online at Amazon or TopStoryLeadership.com

High impact leaders align their habits with key values in order to maximize their influence. High impact leaders intentionally grow and develop themselves in an effort to more effectively grow and develop others. These *10 Values* are commonly understood. However, they are not always commonly practiced. These *10 Values* will help you build trust and accelerate relationship building. Those mastering these *10 Values* will be able to lead with speed as they develop 360° of influence from wherever they are.

Order books online at Amazon or TopStoryLeadership.com

It's easier to compete when you're attracting great people instead of searching for good people.

Blue-Collar Leadership® & Culture will help you understand why culture is the key to becoming a sought after employer of choice within your industry and in your area of operation.

You'll also discover how to leverage the components of The Transformation Equation to create a culture that will support, attract, and retain high performance team members.

Blue-Collar Leadership® & Culture is intended to serve as a tool, a guide, and a transformational road map for leaders who want to create a high impact culture that will become their greatest competitive advantage.

Order books online at Amazon or TopStoryLeadership.com

Are you looking for transformation in your life? Do you want better results? Do you want stronger relationships?

In *Defining Influence*, Mack breaks down many of the principles that will allow anyone at any level to methodically and intentionally increase their positive influence.

Mack blends his personal growth journey with lessons on the principles he learned along the way. He's not telling you what he learned after years of research, but rather what he learned from years of application and transformation. Everything rises and falls on influence.

Order books online at Amazon or TopStoryLeadership.com

10 Foundational Elements of Intentional Transformation serves as a source of motivation and inspiration to help you climb your way to the next level and beyond as you learn to intentionally create a better future for yourself. The pages will ENCOURAGE, ENGAGE, and EMPOWER you as you become more focused and intentional about moving from where you are to where you want to be.

All of us are somewhere, but most of us want to be somewhere else. However, we don't always know how to get there. You will learn how to intentionally move forward as you learn to navigate the 10 foundational layers of transformation.

Order books online at Amazon or TopStoryLeadership.com

"Sales persuasion and influence, moving others, has changed more in the last 10 years than it has in the last 100 years. It has transitioned from buyer beware to seller beware" ~ *Daniel Pink*

So, it's no longer *"Buyer beware!"* It's *"Seller beware!"* Why? Today, the buyer has the advantage over the seller. Most often, they are holding it in their hand. It's a smart phone. They can learn everything about your product before they meet you. They can compare features and prices instantly. The major advantage you do still have is: YOU! IF they like you. IF they trust you. IF they feel you want to help them. This book is filled with 30 short chapters providing unique insights that will give you the advantage, not over the buyer, but over your competition: those who are selling what you're selling. It will help you sell yourself.

Order books online at Amazon or BlueCollarLeadership.com

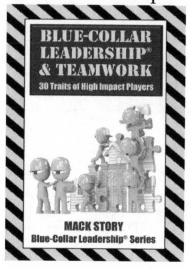

Are you ready to play at the next level and beyond?

In today's high stakes game of business, the players on the team are the competitive advantage for any organization. But, only if they are on the field instead of on the bench.

The competitive advantage for every individual is developing 360° of influence regardless of position, title, or rank.

Blue-Collar Leadership® & *Teamwork* provides a simple, yet powerful and unique, resource for individuals who want to increase their influence and make a high impact. It's also a resource and tool for leaders, teams, and organizations, who are ready to Engage the Front Line to Improve the Bottom Line.

Order books online at Amazon or BlueCollarLeadership.com

"I wish someone had given me these books 30 years ago when I started my career on the front lines. They would have changed my life then. They can change your life now." ~ Mack Story

Blue-Collar Leadership® & Supervision and *Blue-Collar Leadership®* are written specifically for those who lead the people on the frontlines and for those on the front lines. With 30 short, easy to read 3 page chapters, these books contain powerful, yet simple to understand leadership lessons.

**Down load the first 5 chapters of each book FREE at:
BlueCollarLeadership.com**

Order books online at Amazon or BlueCollarLeadership.com

The biggest challenge in process improvement and cultural transformation isn't identifying the problems. It's execution: implementing and sustaining the solutions.

Blue-Collar Kaizen is a resource for anyone in any position who is, or will be, leading a team through process improvement and change. Learn to engage, empower, and encourage your team for long term buy-in and sustained gains.

Mack Story has over 11,000 hours experience leading hundreds of leaders and thousands of their cross-functional kaizen team members through process improvement, organizational change, and cultural transformation.

Order books online at Amazon or TopStoryLeadership.com

"I wish someone had given me these books 30 years ago when I started my career. They would have changed my life then. They can change your life now." ~ Mack Story

MAXIMIZE Your Potential will help you learn to lead yourself well. *MAXIMIZE Your Leadership Potential* will help you learn to lead others well. With 30 short, easy to read 3 page chapters, these books contain simple and easy to understand, yet powerful leadership lessons.

Note: These two MAXIMIZE books are the white-collar, or non-specific, version of the Blue-Collar Leadership® books and contain nearly identical content.

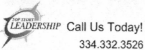

Made in the USA
Columbia, SC
30 October 2020